A WEST COAST KITCHEN GARDEN

A WEST COAST KITCHEN GARDEN

Growing Culinary Herbs and Vegetables

ANDREW YEOMAN

WHITECAP BOOKS
Vancouver / Toronto

Edited by Elaine Jones
Cover design by Warren Clark
Interior design by Susan Doering
Cover photograph by Ryan McNair
Typeset by CryptoGraphics

Printed and bound in Canada.

Canadian Cataloguing in Publication Data

Yeoman, Andrew, 1933–
  A West Coast kitchen garden

  Includes bibliographical references and index.
  ISBN 1-55110-279-X
  1. Herb gardening—British Columbia. 2. Vegetable gardening—British Columbia. I. Title.
SB351.H5Y46 1995   635'.09711   C94-910957-6

To Noël, who makes life bright and full of wonder

CONTENTS

ACKNOWLEDGMENTS

Looking after the garden and farm has taken many hands many days, and I would like to thank the caretakers who, since 1980, have weeded the herbs, fixed the hoses, helped with the lambing and shared our home: Joan Webber, Lorraine Hamilton, Charlie Coolen, Tina Siver, Jamie and Joy Croll, Laura Thompson and Morris Holmes.

Other helpers in the garden include Jan Bate, Nina de Cocq, David Crone, Andrea Ernst, Mark and Sonya Furstenau, Mary Anne Gervais, Leslie Hurtig, Eric and Ian Marcuse, Stuart Mackay, Hanna Masata, Xanthe and Sophie Willer, Kim Williams and my four English nephews, Timothy, Peter, Robin and Matthew, who did yeoman service in the garden for each of their summers at the farm.

Thanks also to biologist Mike Ashwood Smith, George Rostoker, Gerrie Prasing, Dan Jason, Phoebe Noble and Sandra Holloway for sharing their knowledge and to Rachel de Caria for processing the manuscript.

INTRODUCTION

In 1979 my wife, Noël, and I moved from the cityscape of Calgary, Alberta, to the Saanich Peninsula in British Columbia. In doing so we left behind jobs in a school library and a highrise office and the brown high plains with their hot, dry summers and frigid winters to come to the mild moist winters and dry summers of the west coast.

It began on a dreary November day, when we saw an advertisement in our local newspaper: "For Sale, 10 acres of south-sloping hillside overlooking sea and valley. Apple orchard and four-bedroom house on the Saanich Peninsula, Vancouver Island." Noël, who was from the island, thought it might be a farm she was familiar with. It was; we flew out the next weekend and bought the property.

We moved west the following summer. In the moving van were two tarragon plants purchased on Vancouver Island five years earlier. Noël and the tarragon were returning home, while I was off on a new adventure.

Just as described, the land at Ravenhill slopes gently to the south, providing distant views of the Olympic Mountains and San Juan Island; the middle distance reveals a lovely valley edged by Douglas firs and the salt water of the fjordlike Saanich Inlet. The house and garden are 250 feet (75 m) above sea level, which allows the cold air draining from the mountain to pass on down to the valley below, where the Garry oaks wear long beards of Spanish moss.

The topsoil is a clay loam that is 6 to 9 inches (15 to 23 cm) deep. Granite, bedrock or fractured, is never far from the surface and there are outcrops near the house and barn. Of the farm's 10 acres (4 ha), about 8 acres (3.2 ha) is in pasture, reclaimed from a mixed Douglas fir, arbutus and Garry oak forest in the 1890s. Remnants of these trees add character and shade—and tree roots—to the property.

Rainfall here averages close to 35 inches (90 cm) a year, more than half of which falls in four months, November to February. Snow falls most years, but usually no more than 6 inches (15 cm) at a time, and it rarely lasts for more than three or four days. In only three years out of fourteen has there been enough snow to put on cross-country skis.

In the beginning, we determined to keep the orchard going, raise chickens and grow herbs—possibly as a commercial venture. We spent the first year preparing the site for shrubs and perennials, terracing the existing vegetable garden, planting all the culinary herbs we could find, and trying to decide how to alter the house to fit our lives and the developing garden.

The division of labor on the farm quickly evolved into myself doing most of the growing and Noël doing most of the cooking. Other invaluable help was provided by live-in caretakers, itinerant young friends and relatives, and some casual labor in the spring.

By our second year we had the first customer for our fresh-cut herbs; over the years the business became so successful that deliveries took too much time, and we eventually cut back on the number of restaurants we supplied and began to concentrate on selling culinary and landscape herb plants from the farm gate. The vegetable garden expanded and became the site for many experiments with raised beds, cold frames and plastic tunnels, organic cultivation, the rituals of compost-making and growing unusual plants for the kitchen. The apple orchard proved to be so dependent on sprays and so time-consuming that when rabbits started to sharpen their teeth on the capillary irrigation tubes, the trees were pulled out. The chickens were supplemented by ducks (until a large raccoon paid too many visits), five geese and a peacock who came to be called Bluebeard after his fifth wife disappeared. Other inhabitants include two dogs, a cat, a white goat of great charm, a Sicilian donkey and five to fifteen sheep who keep the meadow grass trimmed and provide manure for the garden.

We began writing about Ravenhill because we were asked so many questions about growing and cooking with herbs. Noël self-published a booklet which was eventually expanded into a book, *Summer Delights: Growing and Cooking Fresh Herbs,* published in 1989, for which I wrote the growing section. It was followed by *Winter Pleasures,* published in 1990. Meanwhile, I was writing monthly articles on herbs and vegetables for *Island Grower* magazine, and self-published a booklet called *Feeding Vegetables.*

The farm and garden also serves as a community resource for garden clubs, painting classes and photographers, and students of horticulture, landscape architecture and cooking. This book is the result of fifteen years of growing, reading, experimenting and trying to answer the questions of the many thousands of Sunday visitors who have come to the farm.

The gardening methods are a combination of old and new, many of which have the aim of reducing the gardener's reliance upon harmful and potentially harmful chemicals, and of maintaining or increasing the quality of the soil. The information is directly applicable to gardens of the Pacific Northwest and can be adapted to any temperate-zone garden.

The first part of the book is an alphabetical listing with growing advice for the ninety-plus main culinary herbs and vegetables grown successfully at Ravenhill. The second part looks in more detail at specific subjects, such as plant hardiness, soil testing, mulching, compost and climate modifiers.

I

CULINARY HERBS AND VEGETABLES

The forty-six herbs and forty-five vegetables detailed here have all been grown at Ravenhill Farm. The plants are listed alphabetically by their common names. Specific information includes light and soil requirements, hardiness, pests and diseases, plant and seed sources, and growing instructions.

Plant hardiness is judged according to our experience at Ravenhill and will generally apply to much of the coastal area. Ravenhill is on a gently south-sloping hillside at an altitude of 250 feet (75 m), 20 miles (32 km) north of Victoria on Vancouver Island. The minimum winter temperature is 12°F (−10°C). Frost-free days vary from 230 to 245. The farm is within USDA plant hardiness zone 8 and Sunset's *Western Garden Book*'s zone 5. The hardiness of each plant according to the USDA ratings is also supplied but, as with all such ratings, specific conditions can increase or decrease the chances of survival of marginal perennial plants. Exposure to cold winds, poor winter drainage and hollows that collect cold air are three of the main variables affecting microclimates and the hardiness of plants. Hardiness factors are discussed in more detail in a later section, "Plant Hardiness and Growing Conditions."

Pest and disease problems for each entry are also based on our experience at Ravenhill, although some common problems and their solutions are noted as well. Further information is available at garden centers, botanical gardens, local garden clubs, and from government and educational publications. Most herbs are highly resistant to pests and diseases, probably because of the oils that we prize for their flavor.

Seed and plant availability is based on current seed catalogs. A full listing of the sources can be found at the back of this book.

Note: Entries that follow are herbs; entries that follow are vegetables.

ANISE HYSSOP *Agastache foeniculum* Perennial

Anise hyssop grows 2 to 3 feet (.6 to .9 m) high, topped by long-lasting, purple to mauve flowers in August. Young leaves are green with purplish markings that disappear in full sun. A type with narrower leaves and rose-purple flowers is sometimes available.

Anise hyssop makes a good ornamental. The flowers are seen at their best if surrounded by low plants like the creeping thymes or if six or seven plants are massed together in a large container, such as a half-barrel.

The petals are tasty in salads, soups, desserts and drinks and are used for flavoring meat and making herb tea. The flowers are attractive to bees.

Sun/Shade: Full sun to half shade.

Soil: Not fussy; average to rich. Only needs water in really dry periods.

Hardiness: Hardy at Ravenhill; listed as hardy to zone 4.

Pests/Diseases: No problem.

Seeds: Both seeds and plants are available from Nichols and Richters; seeds from Shepherd's.

Starting: Older plants can be divided in March. It is best to start by purchasing young plants in early spring if you want instant results. Plants will flower the first year from seeding in March or early April.

Growing: Easy care. It can be spindly in full sun and will take a bushier form if grown in partial shade. The plant dies back in winter and should be given a top-dressing of compost in late winter. It is probably a good idea to replace plants in their third or fourth year, as older plants seem to lose vigor.

ARTICHOKE, GLOBE *Cynara scolymus* Perennial

The purple flower spike of the globe artichoke rises to 4 or 5 feet (1.2 to 1.5 m). The huge, grayish, deeply cut or divided leaves arc out from the main stem for 2 feet (.6 m) on each side of the plant. Artichokes are grown for their luscious edible flower buds, but the plant is a stunning eye-catcher in the flower garden as well as the vegetable garden. If, for some reason, you leave a globe until it is too coarse and tough to eat, then you can enjoy the unfolding of the huge, thistlelike purple flower and watch it being visited by bumblebees and butterflies.

Sun/Shade: Best in full sun but will take up to half shade and still produce edible buds.

Soil: Rich, moist, well drained.

Hardiness: Listed as hardy to zone 8 and is almost reliably hardy at Ravenhill. We have lost them to frost one year out of fourteen.

Pests/Diseases: Apart from earwigs, which do not seem to do any damage, the only problems have been black aphids, which can easily be hosed off with a hard spray.

Seeds: Widely available.

Starting: Start from seed, buy young plants, or divide old plants in the early spring. The easiest way is to dig up an entire plant that shows small offsets growing from the base. Those offsets that have some fine root hairs attached can then be cut off with a sharp knife and planted in pots in a shady place. After two or three weeks, new root hairs will have become established and the offset can be planted out in a permanent position. It is also possible to cut away an offset without digging up the entire parent plant. Though I have not tried seeding artichokes, seed catalogs claim that early seedings will produce edible globes late in the first summer. At Ravenhill, edible buds may appear early in April, but the main early harvest is in May and June.

Growing: Our artichokes are grown in a raised bed, spaced about 4 feet (1.2 m) apart and the beds are mulched with compost and straw in the early summer as the ground dries out. The raised bed is very important, for it provides the good winter drainage so necessary for the survival of the plant. Plants need a continuous supply of water and fertilizer to continue producing through the summer. We add compost to the base of the plant in May and June and then water through the compost. Watering should stop in late August to harden the plant off for the winter. In mild winters the younger leaves stay green; in cold winters the leaves die and it may be beneficial to mulch the plants with straw in late October.

ARTICHOKE, JERUSALEM *Helianthus tuberosus* Perennial
The Jerusalem artichoke sends up a central stem 3 to 6 feet (.9 to 1.8 m) high, which in turn divides into a number of flower-bearing shoots topped with small sunflower-type flower heads in late August and September. The tuber is potatolike, but smaller and more knobbly.

The tubers can be boiled, baked, sliced and sautéed or made into soup. The plant is quite ornamental at the back of a border or as a vertical accent in the vegetable garden.

Sun/Shade: Full sun to half shade.

Soil: Average to rich. Not fussy.

Hardiness: Tubers can overwinter in the soil, provided they do not freeze, but it's best to dig them all out (see below).

Pests/Diseases: None.

Seeds: Tubers are available from Nichols and Richters.

Starting: Plant the tubers 4 inches (10 cm) deep and 12 inches (30 cm) apart in the vegetable garden in early spring. If you are growing them as ornamentals and don't mind smaller tubers, plant them 6 inches (15 cm) apart.

Growing: Easy care. In rich soil the plants grow vigorously to 6 feet (1.8 m) or even more; in poor soil with infrequent watering, the plant struggles up to 3 or 4 feet (.9 or 1.2 m) and produces fewer flowers and small tubers. Harvest when the tops die down, being careful to dig out every tuber. The plant can be difficult to eradicate if it becomes well established in rich soil. Clumps of tubers left in the ground do not produce large tubers the following year, so it is best to dig them all out and plant a few again in the early spring. Store the tubers in a brown paper bag in a cool, dark place.

ARUGULA/RUCOLA/ROCKET *Eruca sativa* Annual

Arugula grows to 4 feet (1.2 m), with coarse, divided leaves. The flower spike has small, pale yellow, edible flowers. It is a superb, nutty-flavored salad green and can be cooked in dishes such as arugula and potato soup. It is ornamental when in flower and when the seed pods dry. Birds love the seeds.

Sun/Shade: Full sun to three-quarters shade.

Soil: Best in rich, moist soil, well supplied with nitrogen, but can survive neglect and poor soil.

Hardiness: Young seedlings overwinter at Ravenhill.

Pests/Diseases: Late spring and summer sowings can be attacked by flea beetles—small black jumping insects that make tiny holes in the leaves. Prevention by means of a floating row cover, such as Reemay, is the best answer.

Seeds: Widely available.

Starting: Three sowings of a 4-foot (1.2-m) row in late February, May-June and August-September should provide salad greens for eight months of the year. This can easily be extended into December with the use of a cold frame. Summer sowings, if not made under a floating row cover, go to seed very quickly and the mature leaves soon taste hot and bitter. Reemay keeps the humidity high around the plants and provides ideal summer growing conditions. I like to sow the seed thickly and start harvesting the thinnings when the plants are only 3 or 4 inches (7.5 or 10 cm) high. This leaves some seedlings 4 to 6 inches (10 to 15 cm) apart to mature to large plants.

Growing: Easy care, but does best with daily watering. When the arugula is being cut, weekly feedings of fish fertilizer keep the plants growing quickly. Leaf production can be prolonged by scissoring down the row of plants when they reach 6 or 8 inches (15 or

20 cm) in height, then fertilizing and waiting a week for the plants to grow for further cutting. Leaf production can also be prolonged by cutting out the flowering stalks. I like to let some plants from each seeding go to flower—for their beauty, their edible flowers, collecting seed, and feeding birds. When the seed heads turn brown, cut the pods into a paper bag and store in a dry place. Treading on the paper bag releases the seeds for sowing, making one packet of seeds last for many years. Apartment dwellers and container gardeners can enjoy arugula by sowing it thickly, watering daily, and harvesting it when 3 or 4 inches (7.5 or 10 cm) high.

ASPARAGUS *Asparagus officinalis* Perennial
Underground roots send up edible spears which, when harvesting ceases, grow up into 5-foot-high (1.5-m), fine-foliaged, pale green plants.

The edible spears, appearing in April with the daffodils, announce the coming of spring. The mature plants are highly decorative. An asparagus bed can provide a light-colored edge to the flower garden and a contrasting form to the strong shapes of the vegetable garden.

Sun/Shade: Full sun to one-quarter shade.

Soil: Must be rich and well drained.

Hardiness: Reliably hardy at Ravenhill. Probably hardy to zone 4.

Pests/Diseases: Only the dreaded asparagus beetle, which is like a large, elongated ladybug. The beetles are either orange with black spots or, more commonly, black with red spots. They suddenly appear in May, at about the time that harvesting ceases, and lay tiny sticklike eggs on the spears and fronds. The eggs hatch into small gray caterpillars. The caterpillars do most of the damage, converting healthy fronds into brown twigs. Prevention, by removing and burning dead plant material in the fall, is helpful but not entirely successful. The surest control is five minutes a day with rubber gloves, squashing beetles, eggs and caterpillars. Rotenone, a plant-derived insecticide, is a contact killer with a short, effective life of three or four days. It kills beneficial insects as well as the asparagus beetle.

Seeds: Available from Territorial ('Larac' F1 and UC 157 F2 are two new hybrids that are claimed to be two to four times as productive as other types). Shepherd's sells crowns of new hybrids. If I were starting a new bed I would look for crowns of 'Larak' F1 or UC 157 F2, and if they were not available, I would order 'Larak' F1 seeds. This is theoretical, as the asparagus bed at the farm has been in for twenty years and is still producing enough for a meal every other day during the five-week cutting season.

Starting: An asparagus bed is a major undertaking, but a well-made bed lasts for so many years that a day or two of digging, three blisters and a sore back are a small price to pay. If your soil drains slowly in the winter, the bed should be raised at least 12 inches (30 cm). Double-dig a trench three shovels wide. Fork generous quantities of well-rotted manure or compost into the bottom of the trench. If your soil is heavy, add sand with more organic material. Make a small ridge down the center of the bed and lay each crown 9 inches (23 cm) apart with the roots spread on each side of the ridge. Fill in the trench with a mix of soil and organic material. There should be about 3 inches (7.5 cm) of soil above the crown of the young plant.

Growing: Water the bed every two or three days in dry weather during the first summer. Cut down the top growth when it turns brown in the fall and top-dress the bed with compost or well-rotted manure. The new hybrids allow limited cutting of spears in the second year, with full harvesting in the third year. The harvesting time lasts for five or six weeks, but should stop when most of the new spears become smaller in size.

BALM, LEMON *Melissa officinalis* Perennial
Lemon balm grows to 2 feet (.6 m) in height with mintlike leaves (it's a member of the mint family) and inconspicuous yellow-green flowers. The variegated form (yellow and green leaves) loses its variegation after a couple of years.

The herb is used in teas, drinks and desserts for lemon flavoring. It's very attractive to bees.

Sun/Shade: Full sun to full shade.

Soil: Average soil.

Hardiness: Listed as hardy to zone 2.

Pests/Diseases: None.

Seeds: Available from Abundant Life, Nichols, Richters and Territorial. Plants available from Richters and specialty nurseries.

Starting: The quickest way is to buy a plant or get a seedling from a friend. The soil does not need any special preparation unless it is extremely poor.

Growing: A very easy-care plant. The only care necessary is to prevent it from taking over the garden through its prolific self-seeding. The seedlings are best hoed out when very young or hand-pulled when older. I try to prevent self-seeding by cutting back the plants before flowering.

BASIL   *Ocimum* spp.   Perennial grown as annual

There are too many different kinds of basil to detail them all here. Basils are cultivated in most tropical, subtropical and temperate countries and their culinary uses must be one of the widest of any herb. Basils also play a part in making perfumes and scented oils, and in religious ceremonies.

The basils most commonly grown in North America are forms of sweet basil (*Ocimum basilicum*). At Ravenhill we have tried a number of basils. Opal and Indian basils (*O.b.* 'Dark Opal' and *O. gratissimum*) have a strong clove flavor. Lemon basil (*O. americanum*) is excellent for flavoring fish, but is light on leaf production. 'Purple Ruffles' and 'Green Ruffles', like most of the basils, are ornamental in the flower bed. 'Dark Opal' and 'Purple Ruffles' are great for flavoring and coloring vinegar. All of the basils have done well, but we primarily grow lettuce-leaf basil (*O.b.* 'Crispum').

Lettuce-leaf basil has a sweet but strong flavor, produces a lot of large leaves and makes an excellent pesto (although some pesto purists will use nothing but smaller-leafed forms of sweet basil).

The basils vary in height from 12 to 24 inches (30 to 60 cm). Lettuce-leaf basil reaches two feet (60 cm) in height with a 16-inch

(40-cm) spread. The seed is variable: on some plants the leaves may only be 2 inches (5 cm) long; on others the leaves are bigger than a hamburger bun. It has white flowers in September, or in July if the flower buds are not removed.

The uses of lettuce-leaf basil are primarily culinary. Pesto is as good on toast as it is on pasta. Chopped leaves in almost any dish add taste-bud-tingling drama. However, the aromatic oils providing the flavor dissipate at temperatures above 100°F (38°C), so avoid long cooking and add the chopped leaves just before serving. The same characteristic causes the leaves to lose flavor on drying, and we have found that freezing or preserving in olive oil are the best methods of storing basil for the winter.

Growing basil is not difficult, but the plant needs sufficient heat if you are to enjoy a continued harvest.

Sun/Shade: Full sun for maximum leaf production. Full sun to half shade for ornamental use.

Soil: Basil grows best in a soil rich in organic material. Good drainage is important, and the soil should not be allowed to dry out. Drying out causes leaf growth to stop and encourages flower formation.

Hardiness: Perennial in the tropics, it is a very tender annual in the Pacific Northwest.

Pests/Diseases: Sow bugs may be a problem when seedlings are tiny. The sow bugs are countered by sprinkling rotenone around each seedling when setting out the plants in their summer bed. If the seedlings are attacked by aphids, spray with Safer's soap, making sure to wet both sides of every leaf. When the plants are healthy and growing strongly the pest problems have been few. Minor leaf damage is caused by grasshoppers and green caterpillars, probably from cabbage butterflies. The caterpillars are spotted by the dark excreta left on the leaves and by holes in the leaves; a brief search reveals the culprit. In the past three years a few plants have stopped growing and turned brown, probably from a root fungus. I now burn the plants rather than shredding them for compost, and make sure that the basil beds get rotated around the garden so that no bed holds basil more than one year in three.

Seeds: Lettuce-leaf basil is carried by Abundant Life, Nichols, Richters and Shepherd's. Cook's Garden carries one called 'Mammoth'. Abundant Life, Cook's Garden, Shepherd's and Territorial each have several types of basil, but Richters has the best selection, including Thai basil.

Starting: The first year we grew basil it was seeded in the open in May; it grew well in a hot spell in early June. Then the weather turned cold, the basil went into shock until the middle of July, and harvesting didn't begin until late in August. For serious pesto lovers this wasn't good enough, so we began growing basil in a plastic tunnel. Harvesting starts in the second week of July (June in 1994) and finishes toward the end of August. The tunnel cover is taken off in late July, when the plants have become too large and the night temperatures are warm enough.

A serious pesto habit for a family requires ten or twelve large plants. A well-grown lettuce-leaf plant yields about one pound (450 g) of leaves over the summer. Ten or twelve plants under a plastic tunnel need a 4-foot (1.2-m) by 10-foot (3-m) area.

Start seeds in late March to June, planting the seedlings out under plastic from mid-April to the end of June; or buy young plants to set out under plastic in April, May and June. July plantings are normally fine without a plastic cover.

One successful seeding method is to start a tray full of soil blocks made with a moistened, soilless, peat-based potting mix. A soil-block-maker (available from some nurseries and garden supply stores) is an invaluable tool if you grow many seedlings. Small plastic or compressed peat plant pots can be substituted. Sow two or three seeds in each block or pot. Push each seed 1/8 inch (.3 cm) into the soil, or lightly cover with a sprinkling of sieved peat moss. Put the tray inside a clear plastic bag, keeping the bag 2 or 3 inches (5 to 7.5 cm) above the soil surface. Place the tray over a source of heat, such as a radiator or the top of a fridge. An ideal temperature is 80°F (26°C). The seeds should germinate in three days. The plastic trays used at Ravenhill measure 10 by 20 inches (25 by 50 cm), hold 50 soil blocks and have a fitted, reusable clear plastic cover.

When the seedlings show a leaf, take off the plastic and place the tray close to a bright, sunny window. The plants will get straggly if there is too little light. Rotate the tray 180 degrees every three days so that the plants grow straight. Keep the soil moist but not soggy. The temperature should not drop below 50°F (10°C) at night; normal house temperatures are fine for the daytime.

Sowing directly into soil blocks or pots seems to prevent damping off—that is, when crowded tiny seedlings suddenly keel over. When the plants start to grow their second set of leaves, the weaker plants can be removed, leaving one in each block.

Tiny seedlings are easy to transplant as soon as the first set of leaves is well developed. First, moisten the potting mix, then insert a knife or dibber to loosen the soil on the sides of the single root. Grasp a leaf tenderly and remove the seedling, planting it immediately into a new pot or soil block. Make sure to prepare a hole for the seedling before you start. Firm the potting mix gently around the seedling. Any damage to the stem at this stage is fatal.

After four weeks the plants should be 2 to 4 inches (5 to 10 cm) high, and they can either be potted up to a larger container for growing in a greenhouse or cold frame or set out in the garden under a plastic tunnel. If there is no fertilizer in the potting soil mix, feed the seedlings every week with a half-strength solution of fish fertilizer. If there is fertilizer in the mix, start feeding three or four weeks after germination.

Plant out as early as April. The bed, preferably raised, should contain good soil, well enriched with organic material (leaf mold and compost, steer manure or aged manure). Set the seedlings 12 inches (30 cm) apart. I always set the plants in a small furrow or depression so that watering directs moisture to the roots of the plants. The young plants should be watered in after planting and, if you have many sow bugs, dust rotenone lightly around each plant. This will keep the sow bugs away for the three or four days it will take for the plant to become well established.

Growing: Under the tunnel, depending on the water-holding capacity of your soil, the plants will need watering about every three days; two if your soil is very sandy and fast-draining, four if your soil has a high clay content. I use a watering wand so that the water can be directed to the base of each plant below the leaves. The topsoil should not be allowed to dry out completely.

When the plants are 6 or 8 inches (15 to 20 cm) high, pinch back the tops to make the plant bush out. This procedure also provides the first taste of the joys to come. Harvesting from a late March seeding and a late April planting-out normally starts about mid-July. If the plants are strong and healthy the main growth points and the leaves immediately below the growth points can be cut out every week or ten days. It is important to prevent basil from flowering, as this stops the production of leaves. A cluster of small, pointed leaves just below each growth point indicates that flower buds are forming. These clusters should be removed and can be used in the kitchen.

At Ravenhill the 250 plants under the tunnels get cut heavily one week and lightly the next. When heavy cutting starts in July, the plants are fertilized weekly with fish fertilizer. In the first week of August the soil around each plant is top-dressed with compost. This acts as a mild fertilizer at each watering and also protects the delicate surface root hairs which are exposed by frequent watering. Plants that are lightly harvested require much less fertilization.

In late July the plants get too big for the tunnels, so the plastic sheeting is removed. In September the plants devote all their energy to flower production and it is hard to keep up with removing the flower buds. Leaf production slows down and the growth points blacken as the temperature drops. The plants are pulled out late in September and replaced by a winter cover crop of rye grass or hairy vetch and field peas.

One year we put the plastic sheet back on in early September. This did increase leaf production slightly, but it was balanced by leaf damage from touching the plastic. We have also tried bringing mature basil plants into the house for the winter. This prolongs leaf growth into November, but after that artificial light is necessary for continued growth. Small-leafed basils seem to do better indoors than the lettuce-leaf type. Growing basil through the winter with grow-lights and sufficient heat can be done, but fungal problems may require extensive use of fungicides. If heated greenhouse growing is attempted it may be better to grow repeated plantings of seedlings and cut them when they are 4 or 5 inches (10 cm to 12.5 cm) high.

BAY, SWEET *Laurus nobilis* Evergreen shrub or small tree
Sweet bay grows to about 15 feet (4.5 m) in the Pacific Northwest, but it can be kept to any desired height with pruning. It's shrubby

when trimmed or cut back by frost, but is easy to trim into a "standard" shape, that is, with a branchless lower stem or trunk and a bushy top.

Bay is widely used for flavoring soups, stews and sauces. It's an excellent ornamental container shrub that can withstand house temperatures in winter.

Sun/Shade: Full sun to three-quarters shade.

Soil: Likes a slightly acidic soil but does not seem to be fussy. Average garden soil is adequate.

Hardiness: The top growth is reliably hardy in sheltered locations in zone 8. The roots seem to be hardy to about 10°F (−12°C). Unsheltered plants in zone 8, except in a particularly warm microclimate, do not last long before being cut back to the ground by frost. The best locations are close to the west or southwest side of a house where there is protection from the desiccation and cold brought by a north or northeast wind.

At Ravenhill we planted a second-year bay shrub in a fairly sheltered area away from the house; it lasted for five years in the ground, but was cut back to soil level by frost three winters out of the five. It survived to be transplanted into a handsome pot, where it has lived productively for the past three years; we put it into the garden in April and into an unheated greenhouse in October.

Pests/Diseases: In the greenhouse or house, bay is liable to scale and its associated black mold. Scale is usually seen as a pale brown, round, flattened object up to 1/8 inch (.3 cm) across, attached to the underside of a leaf along a rib or a vein. The insect can be removed with a fingernail or dabbed with a Q-tip dipped in alcohol. Gerrie Prasing, a wholesale grower, grows her bays in a heated greenhouse over winter and uses the following recipe to get rid of scale. To one gallon (4 L) lukewarm water, add 1 cup (250 mL) Safer's Trounce and 1/2 cup (125 mL) alcohol. Dip a cloth in the mixture and wipe the stem and each leaf. Safer's Trounce contains pyrethrin, the pesticide derived from pyrethrum flowers. Rubber gloves should be worn.

Seeds: Richters sells both seeds and plants.

Starting: It is best to buy a plant. Bay can be started from seeds and cuttings, but the process requires bottom heat and patience.

Growing: Easy care if you have the right site. Young plants need watering through dry periods; established plants need little care. The shrub can become straggly without pruning and it reacts well to hard pruning and shaping. An annual spring top-dressing of compost and leaf mold is adequate fertilization for garden-grown plants. Container plants like a peat-based potting soil with some perlite or vermiculite added. We top-dress the containers every spring with a rich compost and provide liquid fish fertilizer at least every month through the growing season. Plants do not need fertilizer during the winter unless they are growing strongly. The soil should not be allowed to dry out.

BEANS, BROAD *Vicia faba* Annual

The broad or fava bean has been cultivated since the Bronze Age in Europe and probably earlier in Egypt and the East. Its height varies between 4 to 5 feet (1.2 to 1.5 m); some are smaller. It has large, fat seed pods and seeds.

The beans are shelled and, when young, can be eaten raw, steamed or stir-fried in olive oil, with shallots and sprigs of mint. The older shelled bean seeds have a tough cover which is usually removed before eating.

Sun/Shade: Best in full sun.

Soil: Average to rich garden soil; a fast-draining raised bed is ideal.

Hardiness: Very hardy. Fall sowings overwinter well at Ravenhill in two winters out of three.

Pests/Diseases: Black aphids can be a serious problem in late May or June. It is a good idea to nip off the top 3 inches (7.5 cm) of each plant, either after the lower bean pods have started to develop or when you first see clusters of black aphids on the growing tips.

Seeds: Several kinds are available from Abundant Life, Nichols, Territorial and Salt Spring Seeds, which has the best selection.

Starting: Crops are sown in November for harvesting in May and June. Beans sown in late February and March will be ready in June and are more liable to have serious aphid damage.

Growing: Very easy care. The plants benefit from an application of blood meal or fish fertilizer in late February (mid-March for beans sown in February). This provides nitrogen at a time when the soil is too cold for the plants to get much nitrogen from bacterial activity in the soil.

BEANS, BUSH *Phaseolus vulgaris* Annual
BEANS, RUNNER *P. coccineus* Perennial grown as annual
Unlike broad beans, the bush and runner beans are native to the Americas and were brought to Europe in the sixteenth century. There is considerable confusion over the naming of beans. Some bush beans are variously called string, wax, snap and green beans. There are also a number of pole, or climbing, forms of bush beans. Dry, or shelling, beans are also a form of bush bean. The runner bean is slightly hardier than the bush bean but requires similar growing conditions. And the soya bean is not a bean at all.
Sun/Shade: Best in full sun.
Soil: Average to rich garden soil.
Hardiness: Tender.
Pests/Diseases: Our bush beans have suffered one severe black aphid attack in fourteen years. After one picking the plants had to be destroyed. Most diseases can be prevented by destroying the old plants after harvest, by rotating the beans around the garden, and by watering the soil and not the leaves.
Seeds: Seed houses carry a wide array of beans—bush, pole and shelling types. Abundant Life and Salt Spring Seeds have a wonderful selection of untreated, open-pollinated, heirloom beans. (Saltspring carries soya, lima and adzuki beans; Nichols carries lima beans; and Abundant Life carries soya beans.)
Starting: These beans do not germinate well in cold soils and I find indoor germination in soil blocks to be a good way of getting an early harvest. The soil blocks are seeded in late April and set out in mid-May when the first leaves have developed. The main crop can be sown in late May or sometimes earlier, but the timing is dependent on the weather, and even early June sowings may struggle and fail.

Runner beans can be seeded or set out slightly earlier than bush beans. They germinate more slowly and grow better in cold ground. In the past few years I have grown some scarlet runners mixed with white-flowered Italian climbers: eight plants twine up 8-foot-high (2.4-m) bamboo canes in the form of a tipi, anchored against the wind by one 6-foot (1.8-m) metal fence post. The poles are tied together about 6 1/2 feet (2 m) above the ground.

In most years I sow a second small bed of bush beans in early July for a late August and September harvest.

Growing: Easy care. On our dry hillside they need watering every three days in dry weather. It is especially important to water copiously when the blossoms show. Bush beans are at their tender best when harvested very young. They grow so fast that harvesting every second day may be necessary.

Dry, or shelling, beans can be eaten when young, but most are grown for harvesting and storage when dry. We have only grown them once at Ravenhill, and they were harvested in late September and stored for winter use. Good sources of information for gardeners wishing to grow these valuable sources of protein and fiber are the Abundant Life and Salt Spring Seeds catalogs and Dan Jason's book *Greening the Garden*.

BEE BALM/BERGAMOT/OSWEGO TEA

Monarda didyma Perennial

Bee balm is an upright plant growing to 3 or 4 feet (.9 or 1.2 m). It bears red to pink to purple flowers in August; white-flowered types are sometimes available.

As its name suggests, the plant is attractive to bees. Its leaves and flowers are used in salads, tea and potpourri. It is an attractive dried flower and is ornamental in the flower or vegetable garden.

Sun/Shade: Full sun to half shade.

Soil: Average to rich garden soil, but it should not be allowed to dry out.

Hardiness: Listed as hardy to zone 3.

Pests/Diseases: Good air circulation is important to control mildew.

Seeds: Seeds are available from Nichols and Richters.

Starting: Divide old plants in late winter/early spring or as soon as new leaves appear. Named cultivars are widely available at nurseries, the best red being 'Cambridge Scarlet'. Group the plants in threes or fives to form a noticeable cluster, spacing them 6 to 8 inches (15 to 20 cm) apart.

Growing: Easy care. If the plants are pinched back when they are 10 or 12 inches (25 or 30 cm) high, the plants will be more bushy and will flower slightly later.

BEETS *Beta vulgaris* ssp. *vulgaris* Annual or biennial

This year-round root vegetable with its delicious young leaves is a staple in the garden. Four of our favorite dishes come from the earthy beet: borscht, baked beets, sliced beets in tarragon vinegar and steamed young beet greens.

Sun/Shade: Full sun is best.

Soil: Average garden soil with some dolomite lime and compost added.

Hardiness: Can be sown in April for a summer crop and early July for a winter crop.

Pests/Diseases: Leaf miner is a problem at Ravenhill. Growing beets under Reemay, or a similar floating row cover, prevents the insect from getting to the leaves. If the infestation is not too severe, the affected leaves can be cut off and destroyed.

Seeds: Widely available. 'Winterkeeper', one of the best overwintering types, is carried by Abundant Life and Territorial. Cook's Garden strongly recommends 'Long Season' for winter storage, but I have not tried it.

Starting: At Ravenhill, we grow beets primarily for the winter root crop, which also sprouts new leaves for eating in the late winter and early spring. 'Winterkeeper' is soaked in damp paper towelling for three or four days, or until the tip of the root appears. The seeds are unusual in that they are compound with two or three seeds clumped together. Soaking speeds up germination in the dry soil of early July.

Growing: Unless a forest of seedlings has germinated, thinning is a matter of how large you want the beets to grow. If you love small, tender beets and greens and don't want 4- or 5-inch-wide (10- to

12.5-cm) keepers, then very little thinning may be necessary. If you are growing keepers for the winter, thinning to 4 inches (10 cm) apart is desirable.

During our first few years of growing beets, leaves damaged by leaf miner were removed every week. The leaf miner burrows inside the leaves, leaving a light-colored trail; most or all of the leaf will then turn brown. Cutting off even half the leaves did not prevent the beets from developing to a good size. In the last three years the beets have been grown under Reemay. This aids germination and early growth, prevents leaf miner damage, and gives some winter protection from frost.

The seedlings should be kept growing strongly by watering every two or three days. Our beets are left in the ground and harvested through the winter, protected by 4 to 6 inches (10 to 15 cm) of sawdust. The protection provided by Reemay is only adequate in a mild winter.

BORAGE *Borago officinalis* Annual

Bushy and soft-stemmed, with large, coarse, hairy leaves, the plant grows to 3 feet (.9 m) high with a similar spread. Star-shaped blue flowers appear from April to September. There is a hard-to-find white-flowered form.

The sprouts and first set of leaves are excellent in salads, having a mild cucumber flavor. The flowers are edible; they don't have much flavor, but they are wonderfully decorative. The plant attracts bees and is an attractive ornamental.

Sun/Shade: Full sun to three-quarters shade.

Soil: Almost any.

Hardiness: An annual that germinates in cold March soils. Young plants frequently overwinter in zone 8.

Pests/Diseases: None.

Seeds: Widely available.

Starting: Seed in place in early spring, or buy one plant and let it self-seed. You can transplant seedlings from a friend's garden, but they must be very young as the tap root is deep and delicate.

Growing: Borage is such an easy, hardy plant and such a vigorous self-seeder that the gardener's main decision is where to allow it to grow. The self-seeded plants are easy to see and easy to control with a hoe. Once the taproot has been cut just below the soil surface, the plant will not regrow. Borage brightens up dull corners and edges of the vegetable and flower garden. A year after first planting, the blue flowers are borne from April to October. Self-seeded plants from late in the summer survive most winters here and reach their full size in May and June. Full-grown plants tend to flop over onto other plants and paths, but they are easy to pull out by hand (wear gloves to protect against the fine bristles), and can then be composted.

BROCCOLI, 'PURPLE SPROUTING' *Brassica oleracea* Biennial
This broccoli produces coarse, purple-green leaves and attractive yellow flowers in May. It grows to 4 feet (1.2 m) tall and 3 feet (.9 m) wide. The harvest starts with cutting off the first small edible flower bud in late February and continues through March and April, when the plant is covered with small flower buds.

Our favorite late winter vegetable, the flower buds have a delicate, nutty flavor. They are delicious raw in salads, added to clear soup just before serving, steamed, stir-fried or added to a pasta sauce. The flowers are edible.

Sun/Shade: Full sun is best.
Soil: Rich, well-drained garden soil with some dolomite lime added.
Hardiness: Hardy at least to zone 8. A very hardy, overwintering vegetable at Ravenhill.
Pests/Diseases: Our plants have not been affected by club root or cabbage root maggot. If they are a problem, apply wood ash around the stems of the plants. Rare infestations of gray aphids are washed off with a spray of water.
Seeds: Available from Abundant Life, Territorial and Cook's Garden.
Starting: Prepare the bed by digging in organic fertilizer or compost with some dolomite lime. It is best to start from seed, though plants are sometimes available. Sow seeds in May or June. Our

sprouting broccoli has self-seeded the last three years; the seedlings, which appear in June or early July, are transplanted to a new bed to avoid disease or pest problems. Four plants are enough for a small family.

Growing: Easy care. Thin seedlings to 24 inches (60 cm) apart and grow a catch crop of lettuce or radishes between them. Once the seedlings are established, reduce watering to once every three days. Top-dress with compost in August. The plants appreciate the nitrogen in a watering-in of fish fertilizer in late February. Broccoli stalks and roots need to be split lengthwise or crushed before composting. Territorial Seeds' hybrid broccoli mix grows well for a summer crop, but I have not tested it for winter hardiness.

BURNET, SALAD

Sanguisorba minor (syn. *Poterium sanguisorba*)   Perennial

Under dry conditions, salad burnet is a low-growing plant with leaves to 8 inches (20 cm), flower stems to 18 inches (45 cm), and a width of 18 inches (45 cm).

The young leaves have a cucumberlike taste and are used in salads and to flavor soups and sauces. It's a good ground cover in damp shade.

Sun/Shade: Full sun to three-quarters shade.

Soil: Average garden soil with some dolomite lime added. Like rosemary, it grows well near cement.

Hardiness: Listed as hardy to zone 2.

Pests/Diseases: None at Ravenhill.

Seeds: Seeds available from Abundant Life. Seeds and plants from Nichols and Richters.

Starting: Seeds, or buy plants. It self-sows in moist locations; it may be a problem in a damp border.

Growing: Easy care. The plants get a top-dressing of leaf mold and a little compost each year. The plants need to be trimmed of their dead foliage about three times a year. The flower stems tend to fall over. Cutting them prevents self-seeding and makes the plant produce more leaves.

CABBAGE, CHINESE CELERY

Brassica napa (Pekinensis Group)   Annual

The Brassica family is huge, of world-wide distribution and ancient lineage. This cabbage is like a cross between a green head-forming cabbage and a romaine lettuce. The pale green leaves are not as tightly wrapped as the heading-type cabbage, and the midribs are whiter, wider and much more tender.

The leaves and midribs are excellent in cole slaw, salad, stir-fries or lightly steamed. It matures much faster than head-forming cabbage.

Sun/Shade: Full sun is best.

Soil: Rich, with some dolomite lime added when planting.

Hardiness: Harvest before the first heavy frost of late fall.

Pests/Diseases: Cabbages are susceptible to cabbage root maggots (see Red Cabbage: Starting). Flea beetles may be a problem for spring sowings; cover with a floating row cover, such as Reemay, as a preventive measure.

Seeds: Widely available. This cabbage is listed under a variety of names, including Michihli, Pe Tsai and Napa.

Starting: Grow from seed early in the spring or late in July for a fall crop. Seedlings purchased or planted out in late August will mature in October and November and have a better chance of avoiding pests than the spring crop.

Growing: It is important to keep cabbages growing strongly; they need regular watering in dry weather.

CABBAGE, RED/GREEN/SAVOY

Brassica oleracea (Capitata Group)   Annuals and biennials

The head-forming cabbages (red, green and crinkly-leaved savoy) are easily grown for fall and winter harvesting.

Sun/Shade: Full sun is best.

Soil: Rich, with some dolomite lime added when planting.

Hardiness: Head-forming cabbages vary in their ability to survive coastal winters; refer to seed catalogs rather than seed packages.

Pests/Diseases: See Cabbage entry above.

Seeds: Widely available, but it is a good idea to choose cultivars tested for coastal conditions (Territorial and Abundant Life). Apart from experimenting with a couple of early spring seedings, I have found it more convenient to buy seedlings in June or July from reputable nurseries. This is an easier, although more expensive, method that fits in well with the freeing up of vegetable garden beds when the shallots and garlic are harvested.

Starting: Prepare a bed by digging in compost with a handful of dolomite lime per plant. Buy plants from a reputable nursery to minimize the chance of club root being imported to your garden.

After planting, firm the soil well with your foot, and spread a 1-inch-thick (2.5-cm) layer of wood ash for 6 inches (30 cm) around the stem. Firming the soil and adding wood ash seems to prevent the flies of the cabbage root maggot from laying their eggs in the soil close to the stem of the cabbage.

Sometimes the cabbage plants are in a pack and have to be separated. The roots should be thoroughly wet before separation, and if there is too little root for the top growth, some temporary protection is important for the seedling. You can prop a piece of plywood at an angle over the plants, staking both the topside and the underside so that the wind does not blow it over on the plants. A second method is to use translucent plastic 1-gallon (4-L) vinegar containers with the top and the base removed. The container is fitted over the seedling, providing sufficient shade to prevent serious wilting. The containers can be removed after two weeks. The Territorial Seeds catalog has excellent advice on growing cabbages.

Growing: See Cabbage entry above. Winter cabbages appreciate a top-dressing of compost, blood meal or fish fertilizer in late August.

CALAMINT *Calamintha nepeta* Perennial

This small, bushy plant grows to 12 inches (30 cm) in height and breadth (less in full sun and poor, dry soil; more in half shade). It bears tubular pink flowers in June and July.

The leaves add a mintlike flavor to sauces and teas and the fragrant flowers are also edible. An attractive ornamental in leaf and flower, it can be used in containers and as an edging plant in the front of the borders.

Sun/Shade: Full sun to three-quarters shade.

Soil: Average to rich garden soil, but does best when the soil is kept fairly moist.

Hardiness: Hardy at Ravenhill. Listed as hardy to zone 4.

Pests/Diseases: None at Ravenhill.

Seeds: Available from Richters.

Starting: Start from seed in the spring, or buy a plant from a specialty nursery.

Growing: Easy care. At Ravenhill it grows in a dry bed with shallow soil and in full sun. It flowers well, but the foliage is low (about 6 inches/15 cm high) and a bit ragged. In a moister location and given some shade it would do better.

It needs trimming in late winter to remove dead stems. The soil around the plants is top-dressed with leaf mold in the late winter.

CALENDULA/POT or ENGLISH MARIGOLD
Calendula officinalis Annual

Calendula is a bushy plant up to 2 feet (60 cm) high and wide with large, pale green leaves. Its bright yellow to orange flowers appear from spring to fall with a few appearing to cheer up a mild winter day. Older plants become straggly.

The edible flower petals are used in salads and for food coloring. It makes a cheerful ornamental that brightens up dull corners of the vegetable or flower garden.

Sun/Shade: Full sun to three-quarters shade.

Soil: Calendula adjusts to rich as well as poor soils and tolerates drought well.

Hardiness: Hardy at Ravenhill. Older plants can survive a winter in zone 8.

Pests/Diseases: Older plants are liable to mildew on the leaves and should be pulled out. Watering the soil rather than the leaves helps to prevent mildew.

Seeds: Widely available. Plants are often available from nurseries.

Starting: Seed in place in early spring, transplant young seedlings from a friend's garden or purchase at nurseries.

Growing: Very easy care. Once established, the plants self-seed vigorously. Young seedlings are easy to transplant but should be carefully watered before moving them. In our area a few plants survive most winters, but they are rarely in good condition and are best pulled out to make way for seedlings. Deadheading the flowers helps to keep the plants beautiful and encourages more blooms.

CARDOON   *Cynara cardunculus*   Perennial

Cardoon reaches 8 feet (2.4 m) with a spread of 4 feet (1.2 m). It has very long, serrated gray-green leaves and thistlelike blue-purple flowers.

The ribs of the leaves, when blanched, are very tasty, particularly when baked with Parmesan cheese on top. The flower buds can be eaten, but they are much smaller than the related globe artichokes. The plant is a great ornamental, either in the back of the flower bed or standing by itself to mark the end of a bed or a change in direction of a path.

Sun/Shade: Full sun to half shade.

Soil: Rich soil well supplied with moisture is best, but the plant can survive neglect and little water.

Hardiness: Hardy with good drainage in zone 8; listed as hardy to zone 6.

Pests/Diseases: None at Ravenhill.

Seeds: Available from Abundant Life, Nichols, Richters and Cook's Garden.

Starting: I have not grown them from seed. We buy plants and set them out in early spring. The planting site should be in a raised bed or have excellent winter drainage.

Growing: Easy care. Keep the plants well supplied with moisture and top-dress the soil with compost in early summer. In September, tie the long leaves to the main stem and wrap with burlap or black plastic. After four weeks, unwrap, cut off each leaf close to the stem and strip off the leafy part from the rib. The ribs can then be used in the kitchen. Cut off the main stem and remaining leaves in the late fall and put compost around each plant.

CARROT *Daucus carota* ssp. *sativus* Biennial

Carrots are in big demand around the farm. The donkey, goat and sheep all enjoy the crunch and flavor of a good carrot. For the humans, carrots are a source of pleasure and beta carotene in all four seasons.

Sun/Shade: Full sun to one-quarter shade.

Soil: Average fertility, but deep and well drained.

Pests/Diseases: Carrot rust fly is the main problem and prevention is the best answer. Provide a barrier between fly and carrot— either a floating row cover, such as Reemay, or an 18-inch-high (45-cm) barrier around the carrot bed. Another preventive measure I have tried is to mound the soil up around the leaves as the carrots grow. This seems to prevent the maggots from reaching the root.

Seeds: Widely available, but the seed you choose depends mainly on your depth and type of soil, and the season of sowing. Cook's Garden, Shepherd's, Nichols and Territorial carry several kinds each. We sow 'Nantes' type, short varieties for our shallow depth of topsoil, plus 'Merida' from Territorial for overwintering.

Starting: The bed is carefully prepared and the surface layer is finely broken up. A small amount of aged compost is dug in. If your surface soil is coarse, the seeds can be sown in a shallow trench and covered with a 1/4- to 1/2-inch (.6- to 1.25-cm) layer of peat moss. Keep the peat moss moist, and germination will be rapid and even. The bed should be thoroughly damp before sowing.

If carrot rust fly is a nuisance in your area, it is best to put your barrier over or around the carrots at the time of sowing. The fly is attracted by the odor of the leaves and lays its eggs on the soil; the eggs hatch into larvae which burrow into the carrots, leaving holes about the size of a pinhead. The best prevention is a floating row cover, such as Reemay, which has the extra benefit of retaining moisture in the topsoil. The retention of moisture speeds up germination in the dry soils of summer.

Growing: Carrots benefit from frequent watering if the drainage is good. If sown very thickly, the seedlings should be thinned twice, the second time when they are just big enough to eat. Carrots do not size up well unless thinned to 2 inches (5 cm) apart.

At Ravenhill the carrots are left in the ground for the winter and covered with 4 inches (10 cm) of sawdust. Like beets, carrots store for a month or more in the fridge, in a clear plastic bag with a few small holes cut into the bag to allow for some air circulation.

CELERIAC/CELERY ROOT

Apium graveolens var. *rapaceum* Biennial

Celeriac has a large—6 to 8 inches (15 to 20 cm) in diameter—almost spherical, cream-colored root; its finely divided leaves grow to 12 inches (30 cm) high.

The firm flesh of the root is used in soups, sliced or grated into salads, or processed into a purée and served as a side vegetable. The flavor is somewhere between celery and parsnip. It is an excellent, hardy, overwintering vegetable that can be dug as required.

Sun/Shade: Full sun for maximum root development.

Soil: Rich, well drained.

Hardiness: It overwinters in zone 8 with protection. In colder areas it can be grown as an annual and harvested before severe frosts.

Pests/Diseases: None at Ravenhill.

Seeds: Widely available.

Starting: Start from seed, as seedlings are rarely available from nurseries. One of my neighbors, George Rostoker, is a source of excellent seedlings. His method is to start the seeds in small flats in late March in a heated greenhouse, sowing the seeds in a sterile potting mix. About a month later, when the seedlings are sturdy and have three sets of leaves, George shakes the soil off their roots, shortens the roots by about 1 inch (2.5 cm) with scissors, and transplants them into 1 1/2-inch-square (3.5-cm) containers. These are then transplanted into rich soil in full sun in mid-May.

Growing: Easy care. Plant the seedlings about 12 inches (30 cm) apart in a well-composted bed. The drainage should be good. I always like to plant in a watering furrow or depression so that moisture is directed to the roots of individual plants. The plants should be kept well watered—at least every other day in dry weather. By late September the roots should be big enough to use. I leave them in the ground for harvesting through the winter under a 6-inch (15-cm) layer of soil and sawdust.

Celeriac root is not very smooth, and peeling with a sharp knife can reduce the size by as much as one-quarter. Put the peeled or shredded root into acidulated water immediately to prevent browning from exposure to air.

Celeriac contains a chemical (furocoumarins) that can cause a minor skin problem on harvesting. The chemical is present in the sap and bruised parts of the plant. If the sap gets on the skin and is then exposed to sunlight, it can cause a temporary brown mark. The same chemical is present in cilantro, dill, fennel, lovage and parsley, all of which have been handled and eaten for hundreds of years.

CHAMOMILE, GERMAN *Matricaria recutita* Annual

Chamomile grows to a height and width of 12 inches (30 cm). Profuse white daisylike flowers bloom from May to October.

It is widely used as a tea herb; the tea is made from the dried flower heads. It has a very fragrant, applelike scent and is a good ornamental.

Sun/Shade: Full sun to half shade.

Soil: Not fussy; copes well with dry, rocky areas.

Hardiness: At Ravenhill, seeds will overwinter and germinate in the early spring.

Pests/Diseases: None at Ravenhill.

Seeds: Available from Abundant Life, Nichols, Richters and Territorial.

Starting: Sow seeds in place or buy plants.

Growing: Very easy care. If planted in a border the plants grow best spaced 9 inches (23 cm) to 12 inches (30 cm) apart. It is a vigorous self-seeder.

CHAMOMILE, ROMAN *Chamaemelum nobile* Perennial

Roman chamomile is a low, spreading ground cover. Its white-petalled daisylike flowers rise 6 inches (15 cm) above the leaves in July and August. It is grown as an alternative to a lawn, and a fragrant tea is made from the dried flower heads.

Sun/Shade: Full sun to half shade.

Soil: Average to rich garden soil which should be kept moist if the texture of a lawn is required.

Hardiness: Hardy at Ravenhill; listed as hardy to zone 6.

Pests/Diseases: None at Ravenhill.

Seeds: Available from Nichols, Richters and Abundant Life. Richters also carries a non-flowering English form which the catalog says is suitable for lawns and pathways.

Starting: Buy seeds and start them in trays, setting out the seedlings in loose, moist soil in the spring. Older plants frequently have offsets which root and can easily be cut off and transplanted in the early spring.

Growing: Loose, moist soil is required if you want a dense mat of plants that can be cut with a lawnmower. In the spring and early summer the plants rapidly fill in the gaps if planted 6 inches (15 cm) apart. Our plants, growing in dry soil, need shearing twice: in late spring and early summer. Plants in moist soil will need cutting more frequently and will require monthly fertilization in the growing season.

CHERVIL *Anthriscus cereifolium* Annual

Chervil's delicate ferny foliage grows to 20 inches (50 cm) in height, with tiny white flowers in April and May. It grows best in the cool weather of spring and fall.

One of the finest culinary herbs, chervil's leaves and seeds have a delicate anise flavor. The plant is an ornamental addition to a shaded garden.

Sun/Shade: It is best in filtered shade but can tolerate full shade. It does not like full sun.

Soil: Average to rich soil, well supplied with moisture.

Hardiness: Very hardy. It sometimes overwinters from a fall sowing. Spring seedlings show in late February.

Pests/Diseases: None at Ravenhill. If leaf miner is a problem, chervil can be grown under a floating row cover.

Seeds: Available from Abundant Life, Nichols, Richters and Territorial.

Starting: Sow seeds in place in early spring and again in late August. If plants are available at nurseries, buy only small seedlings, as older plants go to seed almost immediately and give little in the way of leaf production. The best site is well shaded from strong sunlight from May through the summer.

Growing: Easy care in shade. One way to grow it is to set aside a small, damp area on the edge of the garden where the chervil can be sown once and then left to reseed. This will provide leaves in March, April and May and then again in October and November. To obtain summer leaves it is probably necessary to grow plants under shade cloth. August sowings will provide leaves in September and October. Chervil grows well in a cold frame, and August sowings will provide leaves through December and even later in a mild winter.

CHIVES *Allium schoenoprasum* Perennial

Chive plants have tubular leaves to 18 inches (45 cm) and purple flowers in May and June. Both leaves and flowers are edible, and chives is an essential culinary herb.

The plant is ornamental as an edging or in a border. Giant chives have slightly longer leaves and very attractive rosy-purple flowers. Both forms are appropriate in the flower garden as well as the vegetable garden, but in the rockery will not produce many leaves because they require rich soil and frequent watering. Chives do well in containers, their vertical character contrasting with bushy herbs like oreganos or thymes.

Sun/Shade: Full sun to half shade. Most productive in full sun.

Soil: Best in rich soil that drains quickly and is watered frequently. Chives will survive in poor soil and dry conditions but will not produce many leaves.

Hardiness: Very hardy with good winter drainage; listed as hardy to zone 3.

Pests/Diseases: Occasionally attacked by gray aphids in the fall. The aphids can be killed with Safer's soap. Some of our plants that were attacked by aphids did not survive the winter; perhaps the aphids weakened the plants, or an associated fungus or blight may have killed them. Those plants were destroyed and the bed will not be planted to any member of the onion family for four years.

Seeds: Seeds are available but are slow to mature to cutting size. Plants are widely available from nurseries in the spring.

Starting: It is best to start from purchased or donated plants. Older plants are very easy to divide and grow quickly. To divide mature plants, dig them up and prune the roots to 4 inches (10 cm) long and the leaves to 1 inch (2.5 cm). Cut the plant vertically with a sharp knife into 2- or 3-inch (5- or 7.5-cm) squares and replant them immediately. The operation should be carried out on an overcast day or in the shade.

If you have three chive plants, you can cut one back to 1 inch (2.5 cm) above the ground every week, ensuring a continuous supply of leaves. Cutting the plant back encourages the growth of more offsets and more leaves. If you love the color and delicate garlic flavor of the chive flowers, then you may need another plant to provide flowers.

Growing: The plants benefit from growing in a raised bed, being watered every three days in dry weather, fed with fish fertilizer when a clump is cut back, and given a top-dressing of compost in the very early spring and again in midsummer. At Ravenhill we dig up the plants every three years, divide them and start a new bed.

Chives survive quite well in the house during the winter months, and for a continuous supply of leaves you can pot up one plant in September and dig up a second one after it has gone dormant in late October.

CHIVES, GARLIC/CHINESE *Allium tuberosum* Perennial

Garlic chives are similar to ordinary chives, but with flat leaves and star-shaped, sweet-scented white flowers. There is also an attractive mauve-flowered form.

The taste is also similar to ordinary chives, but with a mild garlic flavor. It's a beautiful cut flower and a fine ornamental.

Sun/Shade: Full sun to half shade. Most productive in full sun.

Soil: Needs even richer soil than ordinary chives and more moisture as well.

Hardiness: Listed as hardy to zone 3.

Pests/Diseases: None so far.

Seeds: Seeds are widely available. Richters carries seeds and plants for both the white- and mauve-flowered forms. Nichols carries white-flowered plants.

Starting: It is best to start from plants. Seeds are slower, but both plants and seeds grow slower than ordinary chives. However, if you need a lot of plants for edging a path or border and have patience, it is much cheaper to start the plants from seed and then wait the two years for the plants to form a good-sized clump. Garlic chives are easy to dig up and divide in the early spring.

Growing: Easy care. A raised bed with good drainage, frequent watering and adequate supplies of nitrogen (compost, fish fertilizer or blood meal) are important if cutting is frequent. In the flower garden, garlic chives grow well with little care except for the cutting out of dead leaves and old flower stalks.

CILANTRO/CORIANDER/CHINESE PARSLEY

Coriandrum sativum Annual

Cilantro grows to 3 feet (.9 m) with fine, dark green leaves. Tiny pale pink to white flowers are produced in spring or summer, depending on when they are sown. Its large, round seeds turn from green to brown as they ripen.

The leaves are fragrant and delicious to many, pungent to others. The plant is used widely for flavoring food in many cultures from Mexico to India. The seeds are used in baking. Cilantro is ornamental in the vegetable garden, contrasting especially well with large-leafed plants.

Sun/Shade: Full sun to three-quarters shade. Seed production is best in full sun.

Soil: Average to rich. The soil needs to be moist and well supplied with nitrogen if good leaf production is required.

Hardiness: Seedlings from fall germination sometimes overwinter at Ravenhill.

Pests/Diseases: None.

Seeds: Widely available.

Starting: Start from seed by sowing in place from late March to June and again in late August. Very young seedlings can be transplanted in moist soil and temporary shade. If buying plants, make sure that they are very young and not starting to flower. Transplanting shock often causes plants to go to seed prematurely. Plants are bushier if spaced 6 to 12 inches (15 to 30 cm) apart. Closer spacing (every 1 inch/2.5 cm) provides a good crop of young leaves.

Growing: Easy care, except you must water frequently if you want more leaves. Fall-germinating seedlings are good candidates for overwintering in a cold frame. (See the celeriac entry for a description of chemicals that may cause temporary skin discoloration.)

COMFREY *Symphytum officinale* Perennial

Comfrey is a low-spreading plant with large, coarse leaves and a purple-flowered stem rising 3 feet (.9 m) above the ground.

The main use at Ravenhill is as a source of potassium and trace elements, either added to the ground directly below potatoes or tomatoes or composted. It is also a bee herb and a tea herb. It is ornamental in flower.

Sun/Shade: Full sun to three-quarters shade.

Soil: It may be best grown in very poor, dry soil to control its invasive habits.

Hardiness: Very hardy; listed to zone 2.

Pests/Diseases: None at Ravenhill.

Seeds: Richters carries comfrey seeds and plants.

Starting: It is probably best to buy a plant, unless some special type of comfrey is desired. Old plants are easy to divide in early spring.

Growing: Our comfrey patch is kept under control by its location in poor, dry soil and by cutting the plants down for compost as soon as the first flower appears. The leaves are left to wilt in the sun for a day and then added to a potato trench or to the compost pile. A certain vigilance is necessary to prevent the comfrey from becoming a nuisance. Its taproot goes deep, and small pieces of root regrow. Like mint, it can be confined in a large container.

CORN, SWEET *Zea mays* Annual

To sow or not to sow, that is the question. Living in the country where corn is readily available from farm stands, it is hard to justify growing this nutrient-demanding, heat-loving, space-filling and water-hungry plant of ancient American lineage. So we grow it for the joy of picking, the pleasure of eating and the knowledge that the stalks can be returned to warm the compost pile and nourish the soil.

Sun/Shade: Full sun.

Soil: Rich.

Hardiness: May sowings require a seed that is tolerant of cold soils, and even then germination may not be good.

Pests/Diseases: None so far at Ravenhill.

Seeds: Territorial carries a number of cold-tolerant seed types. Abundant Life carries open-pollinated types. Nichols carries a wide variety, including ornamental types.

Starting: The easy way is to wait until the soil is warm enough for rapid germination of the seed. In cold springs this may not be until the first week of June. An old English method, I'm told, is for the farmer to lower first his pants and then his posterior to the ground (as a sensitive temperature-measuring instrument).

Because of germination problems with May sowings, I have

taken to sowing the earliest corn in soil blocks in mid-April and putting out twelve plants under a 36-inch by 40-inch (.9-m by 1-m) cold frame in late April to early May. The cold frame top is taken off in late May when the plants are about 3 feet (.9 m) high. The second earlies are also sown in soil blocks and put in the ground in the second week of May. The main crop is then sown in the first week of June. Another advantage of using soil blocks is that untreated seed can be used. Corn seed, especially the early types, from many seed houses is covered with a powerful, purple-colored poison that preserves the germinating seed from death by fungus. Seed houses normally stamp their seed packets if the seed has been so treated. The Abundant Life catalog is the only one that clearly states that only untreated seeds are sold. Quick-maturing corn can be sown at the same time as a slow-maturing corn to extend the harvest season. For example, an early corn like 'Seneca Horizon' can be sown with a midseason bicolor like 'Sugar Dots' or 'Peaches and Cream'.

I like to sow two seeds close together every 9 inches (23 cm) of row with the rows about 1 foot (30 cm) apart. The smaller seedling is later removed or transplanted to fill in a gap. The bed is prepared by digging in as much compost as one can spare, supplementing it with blood and bone meal. Because corn is wind-pollinated, it should be sown in blocks rather than single rows.

Growing: Some books recommend removing the basal shoots that come out from the main stem. I have experimented with doing this but can't tell if it makes a difference. The corn is watered every two or three days in our fast-draining soil, and every second day when the corn is at the silk-tassel stage. A top-dressing of compost is put on in early July. A 6-inch-thick (15-cm) layer of straw put around the plants in mid-June greatly decreases the amount of watering necessary.

After harvesting, the stalks are dug up and the roots and joint-ing of the stems are smashed with a heavy object. Alternatively, the stalks can be split with a spade or sharp knife. Both methods greatly speed up the decomposition of the stalks, which are invaluable additions to the compost pile. The only way I have found to decompose the old cobs is to split them lengthwise. A good shredder would do the best job.

CORN SALAD/MACHE *Valerianella locusta* Annual

The leaves form a rosette 6 to 8 inches (15 to 20 cm) wide and 6 inches (15 cm) high. Small white flowers grow to 12 inches (30 cm).

Its dark green leaves are an excellent winter salad green. It's very popular in France and the Netherlands.

Sun/Shade: Full sun to half shade.

Soil: Rich, well-drained soil.

Hardiness: Late-summer sowings are hardy through most winters at Ravenhill, but are best protected by a cold frame in zone 8.

Pests/Diseases: None at Ravenhill.

Seeds: Available from Abundant Life, Nichols, Richters and Territorial.

Starting: At Ravenhill it is sown in late August for harvesting in late winter and early spring. Sowing thickly and not thinning means smaller plants, but you can often get two cuttings. Thin to 6 inches (15 cm) apart for full plant development.

Growing: Easy care. Water daily until the seedlings are established. The plants really appreciate a watering-in of liquid fish fertilizer in late February. The combination of leaching of nitrogen by winter rains and the coldness of the soil means that there is little nitrogen available to the roots. I have not grown corn salad as a spring or summer crop, but it should do very well under a floating row cover, which will give it moist growing conditions. Corn salad is a good candidate for a winter cold frame.

CRESS, BROADLEAF *Barbarea* spp. Annual

The pale green leaves of this cress grow to 3 or 4 inches (7.5 or 10 cm) long. It is an excellent, peppery winter salad green, more tender and succulent than land cress.

Sun/Shade: Full sun to half shade.

Soil: Average to rich garden soil.

Hardiness: Has survived two winters in a cold frame.

Pests/Diseases: None at Ravenhill.

Seeds: Available from Cook's Garden and Shepherd's, where it is listed as 'Reform Broadleaf'.

Starting: Sow it in September for a winter crop in a cold frame.

Growing: Very easy care in winter. Harvest the larger leaves, allowing the small ones to grow bigger for later harvesting.

CRESS, UPLAND/LAND   *Barbarea verna*   Annual

Dark green leaves form a rosette close to the ground. In May it produces tiny yellow flowers on a 12- to 18-inch (30- to 45-cm) stem. It's a very good, peppery winter salad green.

Sun/Shade: Full sun to three-quarters shade.

Soil: Average to rich garden soil.

Hardiness: Very hardy.

Pests/Diseases: None at Ravenhill.

Seeds: Available from Richters and Nichols.

Starting: Start by seed in the spring or September. It self-seeds in the garden and also does well in a cold frame.

Growing: Very easy care, though the leaves are more peppery under dry conditions. Our original seeding was ten years ago but plants still appear in the vegetable garden. Like all winter greens, it benefits from liquid fish fertilizer in January and February.

CUCUMBER   *Cucumis sativus*   Annual

There are two main types of cucumber: sprawling and bush. Bush types grow up to 3 feet (.9 m) in height and 6 feet (1.8 m) in breadth, but can be contained in a smaller area. The sprawlers imitate the pumpkins and invade the surrounding vegetable beds. They are normally grown on the edge of the garden. I keep intending to make an inclined frame for them to grow on so they can do something useful, like providing shade for summer lettuces. Maybe next year will be the year.

The flowers as well as the fruit are edible.

Sun/Shade: Full sun to one-quarter shade.

Soil: Rich, moist.

Hardiness: Tender.

Pests/Diseases: Sow bugs can be a problem with young plants when first set out. Sprinkle a little rotenone on the soil surface around each plant. This acts as a deterrent for three or four days, by which time the young plant should be growing strongly. Mildew occurs on mature plants. While it has never been a severe problem, it does hasten the end of the fruiting season.

Seeds: Widely available. We often grow 'Sweet Success', and also experiment most years with one other cultivar. 'Sweet Success' is normally carried by the bigger seed houses but we buy two plants from a local nursery. 'Lemon', a most attractive round cucumber, is carried by Cook's Garden, Abundant Life, Shepherd's and Territorial.

Starting: The seeds are started over bottom heat in peat pots in April. The seedlings are planted out in late April or early May in a cold frame. The bush-type stays within the cold frame until late July, when the frame is no longer necessary. The ground is deeply dug and half a bucket of compost is forked in. Two plants are placed in a watering depression in the cold frame. It doesn't seem to matter whether the plants are spaced 2 inches (5 cm) or 10 inches (25 cm) apart. What does matter is that the roots are disturbed as little as possible, which is why peat pots are recommended.

Growing: When seedlings are first set out in the frame, rotenone is sprinkled on the soil. Rotenone is a plant-derived poison which protects the tender cucumber from the sow bug. It also kills earthworms on contact, so it should be used as little as possible. It is important to keep up the supply of nitrogen, so a month after planting I add compost and blood meal or fish fertilizer to the watering depression. This makes a nourishing nitrogen tea every time the plant is watered. Watering is a daily chore for cucumbers, though if your soil is deep and rich and moist, every two days may be enough. Cucumbers should be harvested well before they reach their maximum size so that the plant is encouraged to bear more fruit. The sprawling type of cucumbers outgrow our cold frames in late June. The cold frames bring on the first harvest about two weeks earlier than unprotected plants.

CURRY PLANT *Helichrysum italicum* ssp. *serotinum*
(syn. *Helichrysum angustifolium*) Evergreen shrub
The large-leafed type grows to 3 feet (.9 m) high and 5 feet (1.5 m) across in seven years. It has silver-gray branches and needlelike leaves to 2 inches (5 cm) long and carries pale yellow to yellow flowers in June. It has a currylike scent. There is a small-leafed type with leaves 1/2 inch (1.25 cm) long.

The scent is elusive in cooking. It has been used to flavor baked beans; finely chopped, we sprinkle it on eggs and use it to flavor the poaching liquid for fish. The plant is an excellent ornamental.

Sun/Shade: Best in full sun.

Soil: Average garden.

Hardiness: Listed as hardy to zone 7, and it has been hardy at Ravenhill over the past seven years.

Pests/Diseases: The spittlebug causes minor damage and can be washed off with a water spray.

Seeds: Seeds are not available from most catalogs, and our plants have not self-seeded. Plants are available from Richters and specialty nurseries.

Starting: Buy plants or start from cuttings.

Growing: Very easy care. It needs regular watering only when the plant is becoming established. At Ravenhill it gets some leaf mold each year plus a handful of rock phosphate every three years. Like lavender, it prefers fast-draining soil. If it grows too big for the site, it responds well to being cut back hard; new growth breaks out from the old wood. The seven-year-old bush at Ravenhill had to be removed after sustaining severe damage from being trampled by a cow.

DILL *Anethum graveolens* Annual
Bluish-green feathery foliage grows to 4 feet (1.2 m) in height, with umbrella-shaped, pale yellow-green flower clusters.

Many cultures use the leaves and seeds of dill in cooking. It is ornamental against a dark background, and it is an important host plant for a number of beneficial insects.

Sun/Shade: Full sun to three-quarters shade. Full sun is necessary for good leaf and seed production.

Soil: A rich soil is best, but it will survive poor soil, with poor leaf production.

Hardiness: Self-sown fall seedlings appear in early April.

Pests/Diseases: Aphids are a major problem. A hard spray of water will help to keep them under control. When cutting the dill, the aphids can be shaken off.

Seeds: Widely available. Richters, Territorial, Shepherd's and Cook's Garden carry 'Dukat' dill, a good leaf producer, and Territorial carries a kind grown especially for harvesting seeds.

Starting: Start from seed. While seedlings can be transplanted when very young, most nursery plants will go to seed quickly when planted out. The earliest dill leaf in the garden comes from seeds self-sown the previous fall. The second earliest is from a thickly sown row in March.

Growing: The March sowing can be cut when it's 6 or 8 inches (15 or 20 cm) high, fertilized with fish fertilizer, and watered frequently so that it will provide a second cutting. If aphids cannot be controlled by a water spray, the dill can be grown under a floating row cover, such as Reemay. If you want to collect seed or allow the plant to self-sow, it is important to grow it well apart from fennel, as the two cross-fertilize each other and the flavor of the resulting plants is nearer to fennel than dill. (See the celeriac entry for a description of chemicals in dill that may cause temporary skin discoloration.)

EGGPLANT/AUBERGINE

Solanum melongena Perennial grown as annual

The 4- to 8-inch-long (10- to 20-cm), ovoid, dark purple to white fruit hangs from a hairy-stemmed, coarse-leafed plant about 30 inches (75 cm) high.

The fruit, which ripens in September and October, is used in a large variety of dishes from southern Europe and the eastern Mediterranean, as well as Thailand, China and Japan.

Sun/Shade: Full sun to one-quarter shade.

Soil: Rich garden soil.

Hardiness: Very tender.

Pests/Diseases: No problems.

Seeds: Most of the seed houses carry several types; Territorial has three that are early-maturing.

Starting: I have never grown it from seed; early-maturing plants always seem to be available at the nurseries. The plants get treated the same way as peppers, melons and the squash family. Seedlings are set out under a movable cold frame in early May. The soil is well supplied with compost and the plants are watered every three days.

Growing: The plants will need to be staked, and they benefit from some compost being applied as a top-dressing in July. The top of the cold frame is removed in late July, though it could be earlier if the summer is really hot. Picking the eggplants is supposed to encourage the production of more fruit, but our hot growing season is so short that the first pick in late August or early September is too late for the setting of more tiny fruit. Harvesting continues well into October.

ENDIVE, BELGIAN/WITLOOF *Cichorium intybus* Biennial

The plant grows rosettes of large, coarse leaves and a massive root. The leaves are cut off and a tightly rolled "chicon" or spear forms from the new leaf growth.

The blanched spears are a superb winter salad green, and a good cooked vegetable with a white or mild cheese sauce.

Sun/Shade: Full sun to one-quarter shade.

Soil: Average to rich garden soil.

Hardiness: The roots are hardy through the winter when protected by a 6-inch (15-cm) layer of sawdust.

Pests/Diseases: No problems.

Seeds: Available from Territorial.

Starting: At Ravenhill it is seeded in early June in a bed with a lot of compost. My neighbor sows his in April, with equal success.

Growing: Easy care. The seedlings are thinned to 8 or 9 inches (20 or 23 cm) apart. They need watering every three days in dry weather. In late October or early November the green leaves are cut off about 1/2 inch (1 cm) above the soil surface and the leaves are composted. I then set 8- or 10-inch-wide (20- or 25-cm) boards around the endive bed, stake the boards, and cover the endive roots with 8 inches (20 cm) of sawdust. Do not use cedar sawdust and make sure it is from an uncontaminated source.

In late January check the endive for growth. The harvesting in a normal year starts in mid-February when the spears are 4 or 5 inches (10 or 12.5 cm) long, and continues into April.

My neighbor, George Rostoker, digs up all his roots in early November. He cuts off the green leaves and shortens the roots to 8 inches (20 cm) long and stacks them vertically in peat moss in large plastic buckets, leaving the base of the leaves exposed. The buckets are stored in a cold, lightless cellar. Three weeks before he wants new spears he brings a bucket into a dark room at room temperature and fertilizes the roots with a solution of 20-20-20. So George dines on Belgian endive from late November through until April.

When digging up the endive and recycling the sawdust in April, it is important to dig out the main root mass, as it can regrow from small fragments.

FENNEL, HERB *Foeniculum vulgare* Perennial

Herb fennel comes in two forms, green and bronze. Green fennel has fresh green, finely divided, delicate leaves with small yellow flowers in umbrella-shaped clusters in July. Bronze fennel is similar, but is pale, browny-green in color. Established clumps of both types grow to 8 feet (2.4 m) in height.

The seeds are used in baking and as an after-dinner aid to the digestion. The leaves are used both for flavor and decoration in soups; fish dishes, especially lox; egg dishes; and potato salad. Dried

stalks add flavor when burned on the barbecue. Fennel is ornamental in the flower bed and in the vegetable garden, especially as
a screen or clump at the back of the border. It is also a valuable host
plant for swallowtail butterflies and beneficial insects.

Sun/Shade: Best in full sun, though it does well in half-shade and can
produce leaves in full shade.

Soil: Best in rich, moist, fast-draining soil, but it can survive with poor
soil, neglect, and competing tree roots.

Hardiness: At Ravenhill it has overwintered for the past ten years.
It is listed as hardy to zone 3, but this seems questionable as it is
a native of temperate Europe. Plants cannot stand wet roots in
winter.

Pests/Diseases: None at Ravenhill.

Seeds: Abundant Life carries wild and copper fennel seeds, almost certainly the green and bronze forms described above. Cook's Garden
has a smoky fennel that the catalog states is biennial; it is probably
the perennial bronze fennel. Nichols and Shepherd's carry bronze
fennel. Richters carries green and bronze forms.

Starting: Start from seed, beg a seedling from a friend, buy plants
or divide an old plant. Old plants are fairly easy to divide when
growth starts in late winter. Choose a plant with a lot of low green
growth. Dig out the deep roots unless you want them to grow back
in the same place. Separate off individual, small-growing stems
with some root attached. A sharp knife is the best tool. The offsets
can be immediately replanted if there are many fine root hairs vis-
ible, or kept in the shade in pots until the fine root hairs have
regrown. This should only take two or three weeks. Fennel self-
seeds vigorously, and seedlings to about 10 inches (25 cm) in height
can be transplanted easily in the early spring.

Growing: Very easy care. Plants that are cut often need frequent
watering and should be in fertile soil. If your primary interest is the
green leaves, then it is a good idea to have three or four plants and
cut one to the ground every two weeks. This prevents the plant
from going to seed, which stops its leaf production. Our fennel
plants are usually given liquid fish fertilizer when the plant is cut
right down, and they are also given a top-dressing of compost in
the early spring. If you are short of water, it is a good idea to mulch
the plants with straw in early June.

FENNEL, FLORENCE/SWEET *Foeniculum vulgare* var. *azoricum*
Perennial or biennial grown as annual

The leaves and top stalk are similar to the herb fennel, but given adequate moisture and nutrition it forms a fist-sized tender bulb at soil level.

Grown for its sweet, anise-flavored bulb, it can be used in salads and soup or baked with cheese on top. The leaves can be a substitute for herb fennel.

Sun/Shade: Full sun.

Soil: Rich, moist soil, but with good drainage; a raised bed is best.

Hardiness: Because it only survives one winter in four at Ravenhill, it is grown as an annual. In a mild winter, July-sown seed flowers the following spring and then dies.

Pests/Diseases: None at Ravenhill.

Seeds: Widely available; Shepherd's carries two strains, Swiss and Italian.

Starting: Sowing time is critical; I swear by July 18, but any time between July 10 and July 25 should give satisfactory results. One year the seeds were put in early in March but the plants did not bulb. Dig a 6-inch-deep (15-cm) trench and fork in old manure or compost with some added nitrogen (blood meal or fish fertilizer). Partially fill the trench to within 3 inches (7.5 cm) of the soil surface. Sow two or three seeds in groups, 8 inches (20 cm) apart. Just cover the seeds with soil.

Growing: Water daily in dry weather until the seedlings are an inch or two (2.5 to 5 cm) high. Very young seedlings can be easily transplanted if the root hairs are kept moist. Remove extra seedlings, leaving one plant for every 8 inches (20 cm) of row. The bulb should start to form in September. The row should then be top-dressed with compost (fish fertilizer or blood meal can be applied instead). Continue watering at least every second day if the soil drains quickly. The bulbs should be kept covered with soil, as they increase in size, and they can normally be harvested at the size of a large fist in October or November. If you have not eaten all the bulbs at the time of the first frost they should be covered with 6 inches (15 cm) of soil or sawdust. This will extend the harvest into December unless there is a severe cold snap. (See the celeriac entry for a description of chemicals in fennel that may cause temporary skin discoloration.)

GARLIC *Allium sativum* Perennial

Long straplike leaves rise from the lower part of a fleshy stem. The bulb forms below ground and has eight to sixteen segments. Many cultivated forms do not flower.

The basal bulb has wide culinary and medicinal uses. The bulb segments can be forced to produce edible leaf shoots in the winter.

Sun/Shade: Best in full sun; it will grow in half shade, but bulb development is poor.

Soil: Rich, moist soil, but fast-draining.

Hardiness: Fall plantings are very hardy at Ravenhill. In colder areas, the segments should be planted in early spring.

Pests/Diseases: We take care to rotate the garlic beds around the garden to prevent the build-up of disease organisms. British organic growers suggest four years between onion family crops in the same ground. At Ravenhill, garlic is sometimes planted three years after another onion crop. One year, one or two segments of one-third of the bulbs had small fingernail-sized brown punky patches. Some other local area gardeners experienced the same problem. Local agricultural authorities could not provide an explanation, but the problem has not reappeared.

Seeds: Garlic is grown from the individual segments of the basal bulb. Segments or bulbs are carried by Nichols and Richters (three kinds each) and Territorial. A specialty supplier of organic garlic is Dan Jason of Salt Spring Seeds, who sells twelve kinds. Store-bought garlic may be treated with a chemical to inhibit sprouting and is not a reliable source for growing in the garden.

Starting: The garlic bed should be prepared in September or October with a supply of compost or other organic material with some fertilizer added. Choose the larger outside segments from garlic bulbs and plant them 6 inches (15 cm) apart in rows 8 inches (20 cm) apart. The segment should be set 1 inch (2.5 cm) deep with the root base downward. Segments planted in the early spring do not reach the size of the fall-planted crop.

Growing: Green shoots should appear in December. In the middle of February the plants need a supply of nitrogen. Fish fertilizer or watered-in blood meal are excellent. It is important to keep the leaves growing strongly in the late winter and spring; more nitrogen-rich fertilizer can be added in early March, and the plants should be watered every three days during dry weather. Watering should stop in late May or early June to allow the bulbs to mature for harvesting in July. If your soil is poor, garlic benefits from a high potassium and phosphorus fertilizer in May to assist in bulb development.

When the leaves are almost completely brown and have flopped over, the bulbs can be loosened with a fork and the roots exposed to the sun for a day before the whole plant is taken to a drying rack for storage. The rack should be in a cool, dry place, with good air circulation.

GARLIC, ELEPHANT *Allium ampeloprasum* Perennial

The elephant of garlics is more closely related to the leek than to garlic. It sends a flower stem up to 4 or 5 feet (1.2 to 1.5 m) and has a huge bulb with only five to eight segments.

It has a mild garlic flavor. It's a good addition to soup stock and is excellent roasted or braised with a little wine, or cooked and mashed into potatoes. The purple flowers are ornamental in the flower and vegetable garden, and can also be dried.

Sun/Shade: Best in full sun; it will grow in half shade, but bulb development is poor.

Soil: Rich, moist soil, but fast-draining.

Hardiness: Very hardy at Ravenhill, but it would probably not survive the winter where the ground freezes to the depth of the segments.

Pests/Diseases: None so far, but it should be rotated like garlic.

Seeds: Segments are available from Richters and Nichols.

Starting: Start the same way as garlic, but space the segments 8 inches (20 cm) apart in rows 12 inches (30 cm) apart.

Growing: Similar to garlic, except that each bulb will produce a flower stem, which can be cut off or left on. If you leave the stem, the segment will not be available for eating.

HORSERADISH *Armoracia rusticana* Perennial

Long, coarse, dark green leaves grow to 18 inches (45 cm) high and the plant has a massive root system.

The roots are ground up in a blender with vinegar to make the sauce.

Sun/Shade: Full sun to half shade.

Soil: Average to rich.

Hardiness: Very hardy; listed as hardy to zone 4.

Pests/Diseases: None at Ravenhill.

Seeds: Not easily available. Nichols and Richters mail plants. The best sources for plants are specialty nurseries and friends' gardens.

Starting: Horseradish is one of those plants, like Jerusalem artichokes and comfrey, that have a catch-22. If the plant is given soil of adequate richness for good growth, it is likely to take over the garden. In dry, poor soil the plant neither spreads nor produces good roots. I am experimenting with growing it in a frequently watered half of a whisky barrel, which might even produce a strangely flavored sauce. Old plants are easily divided and can make many offsets. Cut off a piece of root that has a growth point or a green shoot, and replant.

Growing: Very easy care, though good roots need fertilizer and a lot of moisture. When harvesting, it is not necessary to dig up the whole plant—one or two of the massive side roots can be cut off without disturbing the rest of the plant.

HYSSOP *Hyssopus officinalis* Perennial

This small, narrow-leafed shrub to 18 inches (45 cm) high bears blue flowers in July. Rare forms have pink or white flowers.

Hyssop was used as a strewing herb and a medicinal herb. Its fragrance attracts bees. It is used as a bitter, piny-flavored accent in salads, stews, soups and marinades. It's ornamental as a low hedge or in the rock garden.

Sun/Shade: Full sun to half shade. Best in full sun.

Soil: Average garden soil that's high in lime; adapts well to dry conditions.

Hardiness: Listed as hardy to zone 2.

Pests/Diseases: None at Ravenhill.

Seeds: Seeds are widely available; Richters sells plants.

Starting: Seeds and cuttings. Buying plants is the easiest.

Growing: Very easy care. It tends to get woody, but responds well to being heavily cut back in the early spring. It needs little moisture or fertilizer. The plant self-seeds, but not so much as to be a nuisance.

KALE, SIBERIAN *Brassica oleracea* cultivars Annual

The oak-leaf-shaped leaves are green when young, purple when mature. Purple stems rise to 6 to 7 feet (1.8 to 2.1 m). The edible flowers are yellow.

Kale is an invaluable winter vegetable. Leaves are cut raw into salads; cooked in soups, potato casseroles and omelettes; steamed and then lightly stir-fried with shallots in olive oil. It is ornamental in leaf, flower and seed pods.

Sun/Shade: Full sun to half shade.

Soil: Average to rich garden soil.

Hardiness: Overwinters easily.

Pests/Diseases: None at Ravenhill.

Seeds: Available from Abundant Life ('Siberian'), Nichols and Shepherd's ('Red Russian'), Salt Spring ('Russian Red') and Territorial ('Winter Red'). Territorial's description of their Siberian kale does not mention any purple coloring.

Starting: Our first plant was given to us as red kale six years ago and it has been supplying the kitchen by self-seeding ever since. Seeds can be sown April to August; the late sowings will overwinter.

Growing: Very easy care. For maximum leaf production, plants should be thinned to 12 inches (30 cm) apart and watered every three days in dry weather. It is best and most succulent when grown quickly. Harvesting the leaves can start when the plant is 12 inches (30 cm) high. Sometimes our plants self-seed so vigorously that there is a forest of kale seedlings that can be scissored and eaten when only 4 inches (10 cm) high. The seedlings can serve as an edible green manure through the winter.

LAVENDER, ENGLISH *Lavandula angustifolia* Evergreen shrub
The English lavenders vary in size and flower color, from 10 inches to 2 feet (25 to 60 cm) in height, and from pale lavender-blue to pink to deep purple in flower color. Ten-year-old plants can spread to 8 feet (2.4 m) across. Most flower in late June to early July.

Lavender is primarily used in the landscape and for its fragrance. The flowers are also used for flavoring ice cream, jelly and honey, and for decoration. Lavender is sometimes added to "Herbes de Provence," a dried mixture for spicing up barbecued meat.

Sun/Shade: Full sun is best. Plants can survive in half shade, but tend to be straggly and not flower well.

Soil: Poor to average garden soil. Must drain quickly in the winter.

Hardiness: English lavenders are reliably hardy when given good drainage. They are listed as hardy to zone 5.

Pests/Diseases: Minor damage from spittlebugs. They can be washed off by a hard water spray.

Seeds: Richters and Nichols carry several kinds of English lavender, seeds and plants. Seeds often show variations, and buying plants or taking summer cuttings is the best way of ensuring that you get a particular kind. Nursery plants that are simply labelled "English lavender" may exhibit a variety of size and flower color.

Starting: Buy plants, sow seeds in early spring or take cuttings of new growth from an established plant in August or September.

Growing: A very easy care plant, responding well to poor soil and infrequent watering. Old plants can get straggly but grow back well after heavy pruning. Dead wood should be pruned in March. Our plants get a sprinkle of rock phosphate every three years and weekly watering in dry summer weather. If your soil does not drain quickly in the winter, the risk of fungal diseases can be reduced by putting down a layer of sand or gravel under the branches of the plant.

If the flowers are required for potpourri or drying they should be cut just before the peak of glory. Old flowers can be trimmed off after flowering.

LEEKS *Allium porrum* Biennial

This outstanding winter vegetable is used in soup stocks, made into leek and potato soup, braised with a white or cheese sauce, or steamed. It's ornamental if allowed to flower, and is used in dried flower arrangements.

Sun/Shade: Best in full sun.

Soil: Rich and well drained.

Hardiness: Very hardy; listed as hardy to zone 3.

Pests/Diseases: We have had no problems, though it is a good idea to rotate them along with the other onion family members.

Seeds: Widely available. Cook's Garden and Shepherd's carry a summer harvesting type as well as a winter one.

Starting: Growing from seed is a two-step process. First, start your seed in a seed bed or small flat in March for transplanting into a permanent site in April or May. The purpose of the transplanting is to set the base of the leaves 4 to 6 inches (10 to 15 cm) below the soil surface so that there will be a good length of succulent blanched stem. The best soil is well supplied with organic material and fertilizer and drains quickly in the winter.

Young leeks with leaves 6 to 8 inches (15 to 20 cm) long can be bought and planted in May or June for winter harvest. Moisten the seedlings and disentangle the roots. Make holes 1 inch (2.5 cm) in diameter and 4 to 6 inches (10 to 15 cm) deep and space them 6 inches (15 cm) apart in the row (if you like your leeks young, then the spacing can be much closer). A sharpened stake or old broom handle makes an excellent dibber for this job. Drop a seedling into each hole so that 1 or 2 inches (2.5 to 5 cm) of leaf shows above the ground. Watering the seedling washes soil into the hole to cover the roots.

A third source of leeks, primarily for summer harvest, is the small offsets that sometimes form in April around overwintered leeks. These can easily be split off and planted deeply. The depth of planting depends on the size of the seedlings; there should always be some leaves showing above the ground.

Growing: Very easy care. The plants do need regular watering in dry summer weather. Leeks planted in early spring put out a central flower stem in June; this stem should be broken off unless you want it to develop for ornamental purposes. Harvesting can take place at any time after the plants are over 3/4 inch (1.8 cm) in diameter. The plants start to form flower shoots in late March and can then be pulled out.

LEMON GRASS *Cymbopogon citratus* Perennial

The substantial grasslike leaves grow to 1 foot (30 cm) high. Although this plant must be brought into a cool greenhouse in winter, it is worth growing for those interested in Asian cuisines, particularly that of Thailand, where lemon grass is widely used.

Sun/Shade: Full sun to half shade.

Soil: When grown in a container, the soil should be a mix of two-thirds sterilized potting soil and one-third compost or composted steer manure.

Hardiness: Very tender.

Pests/Diseases: None so far.

Seeds: Richters carries plants.

Starting: Buy a plant from a specialty nursery, or start your own from leaves and stalk purchased from a Chinese grocery store. Place the stalk in water, which should be changed every three or four days, until roots develop. The rooted plant should then be potted up into at least a 1-gallon (4-L) container with rich soil.

Growing: We have kept one growing for four years, putting it outside in the late spring and in a cool, frost-free greenhouse for the winter. The plant should only be fertilized when it is growing.

LETTUCE *Lactuca sativa* Annual or biennial

The three main types are leaf, head and romaine. Within each of these types there are variations in the shape, crispness and color (red to brown to green) of the leaves. Each type contains cultivars that are specially suited to spring, summer or fall sowing.

Sun/Shade: Best in full sun. Leaf lettuce is good in full sun to half shade.

Soil: Rich soil, well supplied with nitrogen.

Hardiness: Lettuce is difficult to overwinter reliably.

Pests/Diseases: Small slugs do minor damage, but can be controlled by placing saucers of beer in winter cold frames. Fungus diseases are also a serious problem when plants are grown in a cold frame.

Seeds: Most seed houses carry a wide array of lettuce seeds, but Cook's Garden is the lettuce specialist, with dozens of different kinds, including some of the better European strains that do well in the Pacific Northwest. Abundant Life and Territorial both test their offerings under coastal conditions.

At Ravenhill we especially enjoy the French butterheads and ask travelling friends to bring seeds back. Some of these types have started to appear in the catalogs; for example, 'May King' and 'Four Seasons' ('Continuity'). Other favorite lettuces are 'Winter Density', 'Little Gem' and 'Lolla Rossa'.

Starting: I try to sow at least two kinds of lettuce seed every month. February sowings are made into soil blocks or flats, germinated inside and transplanted outside into a cold frame. March and April sowings are germinated inside and transplanted into the garden. May and June sowings are made in a seed bed or in place in the garden. July and August sowings are made in shade, either in soil blocks or flats, then transplanted to a sunny site in the garden. The July and August sowings can be sown in place in the garden, provided the bed is shaded through the first two or three weeks. If we miss a sowing, we buy seedlings from a nursery instead.

Growing: Leaf lettuce needs little thinning and can be cut more than once. Head and romaine lettuce grow best when placed about 12 inches (30 cm) apart. Transplanting in dry weather is especially difficult as it is very hard to avoid damaging the feeder roots that supply water to the leaves and stem. The reduced supply of water causes the leaves to wilt; this sets the plant back and makes it more liable to damage from insects or diseases. If the plant has a lot of leaves, some can be cut off to reduce the demand for water. Seedlings can be temporarily shaded with a staked board or inverted plastic bottles with the cap removed and the bottom cut out. Shading reduces the amount of water lost from the leaves. The main demand that lettuce makes on the grower is frequent watering once the lettuce is planted out. The ideal is every morning in dry weather.

It's easy to grow lettuce for harvesting from April to November. The winter months are more difficult, and my efforts have only occasionally succeeded. This has much to do with inattention to the winter cold frame chores of maintaining air circulation and watering, and motivation is lessened by the availability of easily grown, hardier salad greens like corn salad, land cress, mustards and arugula. For gardeners wishing to experiment with growing lettuce over winter, I would suggest 'Kweik' and 'Winter Density'.

LOVAGE *Levisticum officinale* Perennial

Lovage has large, divided, pale green leaves with an umbrella-shaped compound flower head. Tiny yellow-green flowers appear on the ends of the 3- or 4-inch (7.5- or 10-cm) spokes of the umbrella. It grows up to 5 feet (1.5 m) tall.

Lovage can be used in many ways. The celerylike flavor of the leaves is a wonderful addition to soups, stocks, stews and sauces. Lovage seeds are used in baking and the first young spring shoots can be eaten like asparagus. It is ornamental at the back of the border, especially when contrasting with darker-leafed plants.

Sun/Shade: Full sun to almost full shade, but best in full sun.

Soil: Average to rich garden soil; best with frequent watering.

Hardiness: Fully hardy; listed as hardy to zone 1.

Pests/Diseases: The leaves are sometimes attacked by the leaf miner. Damaged leaves should be removed and destroyed.

Seeds: Available from Abundant Life, Nichols, Richters and Territorial. Plants are available from Richters, Nichols and specialty nurseries.

Starting: Seed or plants. Second year or older plants are easily dug up and divided when growth spears first appear in March. Each spear should have a piece of root with fine root hairs attached.

Growing: Very easy care, though if you want it both as an ornamental and for cutting the leaves you may need three or four plants. For maximum leaf growth the plants require a rich soil and frequent watering; as well, any flowering stalks should be cut down to ground level. Individual plants may be cut back once or twice during the summer. At Ravenhill the plants are fertilized with compost, blood meal or fish fertilizer after being cut back. In late winter the dead stalks are removed and the ground top-dressed with compost. (See the celeriac entry for a description of chemicals that may cause temporary skin discoloration.)

MARJORAM, FRENCH/HARDY *Origanum vulgare* Perennial
The marjorams and oreganos are all part of the genus *Origanum*, and the naming of the different kinds is extremely confusing. At Ravenhill we grow two marjorams (see the following entry for sweet marjoram) and two oreganos (see Oregano).

French, or hardy, marjoram has the same botanical name as Greek and Italian oregano, causing some confusion. Hardy marjoram is a compact, low-growing, bushy plant to 8 inches (20 cm) high with pink flowers to 12 inches (30 cm) high. It has beautiful fresh green leaves in the spring. It is not invasive.

The leaves have a mild oregano flavor. The plant makes a good ornamental for the rock garden and the front of a border.

Sun/Shade: Full sun to half shade.

Soil: Average to rich garden soil with some dolomite lime added on planting.

Hardiness: Reliably hardy at Ravenhill, in zone 8.

Pests/Diseases: None.

Seeds: Seeds labelled common marjoram and *Origanum vulgare* may not be the same plant as described above. It is best to buy a number of marjoram plants and see which meet your requirements for flavor and form.

Starting: Established plants are easy to divide as growth starts in March. Cuttings can be taken in the summer.

Growing: Very easy care. It is drought tolerant, like most of the *Origanum* genus. Dead flower stems should be trimmed in early spring.

MARJORAM, SWEET

Origanum majorana Perennial grown as an annual

Sweet marjoram has grayish-green leaves on multiple stems to about 10 inches (25 cm) high with knotted, pale greenish flowers rising above the leaves. The plant is not very vigorous and does not produce a lot of leaves until late in the summer.

It is an outstanding culinary herb with a sweet, intense, distinctive flavor that is excellent with fish or chicken, in sauces, or chopped into salads. The flavor can be elusive, and is easily dissipated by too much heat. The leaves are best added just before serving.

Sun/Shade: Full sun. Will grow in half shade, but will have less flavor.

Soil: Average to rich garden soil. Add dolomite lime if soil is acidic.

Hardiness: Tender; usually grown as an annual. It is not reliably hardy at Ravenhill, but it has wintered over in a cold greenhouse one year out of two.

Pests/Diseases: None outside. One winter six plants overwintering in containers in an unheated greenhouse succumbed to an unknown cause.

Seeds: Available from Abundant Life, Nichols, Richters and Territorial. Plants are available from Richters and specialty nurseries.

Starting: From seed or summer cuttings, or buy plants. March sowings should be made inside and moved out to a cold frame before planting out in late April. May seedings can be made in place.

Growing: Very easy care. It responds to cutting by sending out new branches and leaves and it only needs water in very dry periods. As noted above, putting the plants in a cold greenhouse for the winter can lead to the loss of plants, but in a previous year, plants from a June sowing overwintered successfully in a cold greenhouse.

MINTS *Mentha* spp. Perennial

The main culinary mints are types of spearmint (*M. spicata*), peppermint (*M. x piperita*) and applemint (*M. suaveolens*). They hybridize freely, which accounts for some confusion in naming the mints. Two other mints that have some culinary value are Corsican mint (see the following entry) and pennyroyal (see under Pennyroyal).

Spearmint has coarse, wide, pointed, fresh green, heavily serrated leaves and pale purple flowers to 2 feet (60 cm) high. It will be less tall in full sun, taller in shade. It has green, slightly hairy stems and invasive root runners.

Peppermint has finer, narrower leaves with less serration. It grows to 3 feet (90 cm), has pale purple flowers, purplish, almost smooth stems, and invasive root runners.

Applemint has rounded, serrated, pale green leaves and hairy green stems. Pineapple mint is a variegated form of applemint with white margins on the leaves. They grow to 2 feet (60 cm), higher in shade. They are not quite as vigorously invasive as spearmint and peppermint.

Spearmint is the mint used for flavoring lamb dishes; we either make it into jelly or soak the leaves in vinegar. It is also good with potatoes, peas, broad beans, carrots, chicken and yoghurt. It's used for making tea and is a source of flavoring for essences, candy and chewing gum. The plant attracts bees.

Peppermint is mainly used for a wide variety of desserts, and for making tea.

Applemint has a milder flavor and is an excellent tea herb.

Sun/Shade: These three mints can take full shade to full sun; the strongest flavor is produced in full sun.

Soil: The best growth is in rich, moist soil. The best flavor is in drier, average garden soil.

Hardiness: All hardy at Ravenhill; listed as hardy to zones 1 to 4, depending on the type.

Pests/Diseases: About eight years ago a new spearmint bed browned and died back in the late summer. All the top growth was then cut back and burned. The disease, which was not identified but was probably rust, has not returned. The spittlebug causes minor leaf distortions and can be washed off with a hard spray of water. Mildew sometimes attacks the old growth of mints in shady places. Cut back and burn the old growth.

Seeds: Start with plants that you have sampled and whose taste appeals to you. Richters carries a wide variety, including the three mints detailed above, almost all as plants. Nichols carries several mints as plants.

Starting: Start with rooted stem cuttings, by the division of old plants in the spring, by layering old plants, or buying plants at nurseries. All three mints are best started in places where their roots can be confined. Green plastic lawn edging is not high enough to confine the roots and stems, which put down roots where they touch the ground. Large containers like half-barrels are excellent, as are smaller 4-gallon (18-L) black plastic plant pots. We grow mint in five half-barrels and three small raised beds, each with three sides formed by boards and with well-used paths surrounding each bed. The mints in the beds still try vigorously to escape, but can easily be controlled by pulling out the runners twice a year.

Growing: Mints are best started with lots of organic material in the soil. If the soil is kept moist, the flavoring oils may be reduced because growth is so rapid. This can be controlled to some extent by the frequency of watering.

The mints are very easy care and survive well on neglect. The frequency of watering and fertilizing depends partly on how often the plants are cut. Two of our beds that we cut down twice during the summer have been in the same place for ten years. These beds are given a top-dressing of compost in March and again in July. In addition, the plants that are cut each week are given a dose of fish fertilizer. The beds and tubs are watered every three days in dry weather.

MINT, CORSICAN *Mentha requienii* Perennial

Corsican mint forms a very low-growing, bright green mat of tiny round leaves with even smaller blue flowers in July.

It has a very strong peppermint taste and smell, exactly like crème de menthe. It is used mainly in desserts and for flavoring drinks. A very attractive ground cover for lightly shaded areas, it grows well between bricks and paving stones set in sand.

Sun/Shade: Full shade to half sun. Filtered shade is best.

Soil: Average garden soil.

Hardiness: It is said to be hardy to zone 6, but it is not reliably winter hardy here in zone 8.

Pests/Diseases: Not a problem at Ravenhill.

Seeds: Buy or beg plants; seeds are not available. Plants are carried by Nichols, Richters and specialty nurseries.

Starting: Well-grown nursery plants in 4-inch (10-cm) pots can be cut in quarters with a sharp knife and planted in a moist, shady place in April and May. If planted 4 inches (10 cm) apart in fine soil which is kept moist, they will quickly spread together.

Growing: Very easy care, but it needs regular watering in dry weather. The plants normally suffer some winter damage but grow together quickly in the spring. The late November cold winds of 1993, following a period of warm, rainy weather, killed off our Corsican mint except for some sheltered fragments up against a wall. The leaves are so small that harvesting is a surgical operation.

MUSKMELON/CANTALOUPE *Cucumis melo* Annual

Who can resist the fragrance and flavor of a sun-ripened melon? Perhaps you are one of the lucky gardeners with a special heat-trapping microclimate that ripens the fruit without artificial means. Most coastal gardeners are not so fortunate and need some form of frame to capture the sunlight and reduce air circulation.

Sun/Shade: Full sun to one-quarter shade.

Soil: Rich, moist.

Hardiness: Tender; it normally needs protection until the soil warms up in June.

Pests/Diseases: Sow bugs can be a problem for young, stressed melon seedlings. Use rotenone around the young plants as a preventive measure until the plants are established. Mildew is severe in September, but this normally does not greatly affect the plant until after harvesting.

Seeds: Available from Abundant Life (several kinds of heirloom seeds, mainly early ripening); Cook's Garden (mainly early ripening), and Shepherd's (mainly suitable for the Pacific Northwest). The catalogs give the time from seeding to harvesting as a range of between 68 and 85 days, depending on the type of seed. At Ravenhill the average for early-ripening melons is close to 110 days!

Starting: Choose an early-ripening cantaloupe/muskmelon and start it the same way as pumpkins and cucumbers: in April, sow two or three seeds to a peat pot; cover with a clear plastic bag and place over a heating unit to keep it about house temperature. When the first leaves appear, remove the plastic bag and place the peat pot near a bright warm window.

Growing: Muskmelons are easy care, provided the plants get protection from cold, a rich soil and frequent watering. At Ravenhill a half-bucket of compost is dug into a 36- by 40-inch (.9- by 1-m) low hill and two to four seedlings are planted in early May in a central depression. The seedlings are watered in and covered with a movable, wooden-sided cold frame. A little rotenone is sprinkled around the stem of each seedling to discourage sow bugs from eating the edges of the leaves and sometimes even the stems. This provides protection for three or four days, by which time the seedling is growing well and is not so attractive to insects. The soil is kept moist but not soggy, and a top-dressing of compost and blood meal is put on the soil around the plant in early July. The melons ripen in mid- to late August. They do not reach the size of store-bought fruit, but one hill ripens between five and twelve sweet and delicious fruits.

MUSTARD, ORIENTAL *Brassica juncea* Annual
MIZUNA GREENS *Brassica rapa* var. *nipposinica* Annual or biennial
We grow two types of mustard green at Ravenhill, *Brassica juncea* 'Miike Giant' and mizuna, *Brassica rapa* var. *nipposinica*. The plants are strikingly dissimilar in form and flavor. 'Miike Giant' has huge leaves that are green shading to purple and grows to 4 feet (1.2 m)

in height topped by edible yellow flowers. The leaves have a strong Dijon mustard flavor and are used in fall, winter and spring salads as well as in stir-fries and soups. Summer leaves tend to be too strong and bitter for salad use.

Mizuna has narrow, pale green, serrated leaves up to 12 inches (30 cm) long with a crisp white central rib. It has a very mild mustard flavor and can be harvested year round for use in salads, stir-fries and soups.

Sun/Shade: Full sun to half shade.

Soil: Best in rich, moist soil well supplied with nitrogen. They grow in poor soil, but the leaves will not be tender.

Hardiness: Overwinter at Ravenhill.

Pests/Diseases: Flea beetles may cause minor damage in the late spring by cutting small holes in the leaves. If the damage is severe, it may be necessary to grow the next spring crop under Reemay or a similar floating row cover.

Seeds: Seeds of both 'Miike Giant' and mizuna are widely available. 'Miike Giant' is sometimes called 'Red Giant' or 'Giant Red'.

Starting: Start from seed early in March and in August or September. I like to sow some densely for an early harvest of small leaves and grow some thinned to 8 inches (20 cm) apart for large overwintering plants.

Growing: As with most salad greens and vegetables, the aim should be to keep them growing without stops from underwatering or poor soil. Incorporate compost with added nitrogen in the soil before sowing and add nitrogen when you start to cut. If you leave a few plants to go to seed, 'Miike Giant' and mizuna self-sow readily. Harvesting can begin when the leaves are only a few inches long, in which case the plant will grow more leaves for further cutting in two weeks.

ONIONS *Allium cepa*

Biennial, sometimes perennial, usually grown as annual

There are so many different kinds of onions that it can be confusing to the grower. At Ravenhill, we grow three main types. There are those that make large bulbs, of which there are three forms: storage, sweet Spanish and overwintering sweet Spanish. Storage onions keep the best and are the most pungent. Sweet Spanish are mild and sweet and keep for about four months. The overwintering sweet Spanish, like 'Walla Walla', are even sweeter and are great for spicing up a hamburger, but they don't keep well.

The second kind is variously called scallions or bunching, green, multiplier, or spring onion (see Onions, Bunching, below). These form a small, crisp, white basal part with edible green shoots. The third kind is the perennial Welsh onion, *Allium fistulosum,* listed below.

ONIONS, BULB *Allium cepa* (Cepa Group)

Sun/Shade: Need full sun for good bulb development.

Soil: Fertile soil, high in organic matter.

Hardiness: The storage and sweet Spanish onions are grown as annuals; 'Walla Walla' can overwinter in zone 8, but it has not been completely reliable at Ravenhill. Good drainage and a late February application of nitrogen-rich fertilizer are important for growing the overwintering onions.

Pests/Diseases: No problem yet at Ravenhill, though all members of the onion family are carefully rotated to prevent the build-up of disease problems. Beds are planted with members of the *Allium* genus every third year only.

Seeds: Seeds, sets and seedlings are widely available. Sets are the small, whole, red or yellow onion bulbs that many nurseries carry in the spring. Each small bulb grows into a much larger one for harvesting in July or August. Sets are easy to grow but have the reputation of sending up a flower spike. In my experience this is not common, but the sets do not seem to make as big a bulb as a seedling. Territorial has several overwintering onions, including 'Walla Walla', that are sown in August for harvesting the following June.

Starting: If you wish to harvest storage or Spanish onions of large size from seed, it is best to start them indoors in February, planting them out in a permanent bed in March. Most years we buy seedlings, occasionally sets, and plant them in rich soil in April or early May. One year we sowed 'Walla Walla' in late July. Half the plants survived the winter; the flavor and sweetness of the harvested onions were outstanding.

Growing: Storage and Spanish onions appreciate frequent watering in dry periods in the spring, but watering should be cut back in July until harvest. Bend the leaves over when they are half brown and pull the bulbs when the necks start to go brown. Leave the roots exposed to the sun for half a day. Store the bulbs in a warm, dry place until the leaves and the stem can be rubbed off. The bulbs can then be kept in a cool, dry, airy place until the chef requires them.

ONIONS, BUNCHING   *Allium cepa* (Aggregatum Group)
Sun/Shade: Best in full sun but do well in half shade.
Soil: Average to rich garden soil.
Hardiness: They are grown as annuals but also provide a good winter harvest from a September planting in a cold frame.
Pests/Diseases: No problems yet, though crop rotation is an important preventive measure, with *Allium* species planted in a bed only every third year.
Seeds: You can start these onions by sowing seed or planting sets or small bulbs (see Onions, Bulb). Bunching onion bulbs are widely available, although there are some differences between garden writers and seed catalogs as to what exactly the names multiplier, bunching, spring and scallion mean.
Starting: Plant the bulbs or seeds in March or as soon as the ground can be worked. The bulbs are fast growing and are good fillers between slower growing plants.
Growing: Easy care. Water in dry periods, and harvest one clump at a time, starting when the leaves are 6 inches (15 cm) long. Leave a few clumps in the ground so that the bulbs will get large and mature. When the leaves die back, dig up and separate the clump and replant some bulbs immediately, or dry and store them to plant the following year.

ONION, WELSH *Allium fistulosum* Perennial

Welsh onion has stout, tubular leaves and stems that grow to 3/4 inch (.8 cm) wide and 32 inches (80 cm) high; creamy white flower heads appear in June. The leaves grow from small basal swellings and can be harvested through most winters.

The leaves, chopped like chives, give a strong onion flavor to soups, stir-fries, stews and salads. This plant is especially useful when the chives are hibernating. It is an ornamental vertical accent in a border, at its best with a dark background.

Sun/Shade: Full sun to half shade.

Soil: Average to rich garden soil.

Hardiness: Hardy at Ravenhill. The top growth is almost always hardy to zone 8; the bulbs are listed as hardy at least to zone 3.

Pests/Diseases: None so far.

Seeds: Catalog listings are not always reliable. Abundant Life lists an evergreen, bunching or scallion Welsh onion, which may be an *Allium fistulosum*. Nichols lists a Welsh onion, but although identified as *A. fistulosum* the description does not match the plant grown at Ravenhill. Richters' Welsh onion is listed as *A. fistulosum*. A further complication is that the term Welsh does not refer to Wales; it comes from the German word "walsch," meaning "foreign."

Starting: Buy plants from a specialty nursery or seeds from Richters. Seeds take a year to produce much in the way of cuttable stems. Self-sown seeds germinate readily in the fall.

Growing: Very easy care. The bulbs increase in number quite slowly, unlike shallots or garlic. After two or three years there may be twenty or more bulbs in a clump and the clump should be dug up and some bulbs replanted.

OREGANO *Origanum vulgare* Perennial

Because of identification and hybridizing problems it may be easiest to use "white-flowered" and "purple-flowered" as the common names for the culinary oregano. At Ravenhill we call the white-flowered form Greek and the purple-flowered form Italian, with little justification.

Both grow to 30 inches (75 cm) in height in full sun. The white-flowered form has pale green outer coverings for the flowers; the purple-flowered form has purple outer parts. There are also pink-flowered plants that appear to be intermediate between the white and the purple. All have similar leaves and stems, though some of the purple plants show darker leaves and purplish stems. The stems of all are hairy; some of the white-flowered plants are hairier than the purple. These oreganos can be invasive in the garden.

The flavor of the white-flowered form is the strongest and can give a numbing sensation to the tongue. The pink-flowered form is also stronger than the purple. The white- and pink-flowered forms are preferred by chefs specializing in Mediterranean cooking. Oregano is identified with pizza and other dishes with tomato sauces, but it is used with many cheese and egg combinations, meats and vegetables, garlic and olive oil.

Oregano is an attractive ornamental and the purple flowers dry well.

Sun/Shade: Best in full sun. It can take half shade, but has less flavor.

Soil: Average to rich garden soil. It should be well drained and the addition of dolomite lime is beneficial if your soil is acidic.

Hardiness: Both are hardy at Ravenhill when grown in raised beds.

Pests/Diseases: Individual stems occasionally die back and should be cut out and burned. This rarely affects the whole plant and does not seem to spread. Spittlebugs may suck the juices of the plant, but the damage is minor and the spittle can be washed off with a hard spray.

Seeds: It's best to buy plants. Nichols and Richters carry plants; Richters has the wider selection.

Starting: Old plants are easily divided in the early spring as the new growth starts. Cuttings can be taken in the summer. The plants set a lot of seeds, but they are usually variable and need careful selection to maintain a particular form. Oregano is a good subject for layering, as the lower stems root easily. Pin the stem to the soil with bent wire or a stone; it helps to put peat moss around the stem at the potential rooting point. The peat moss and soil should be kept damp until the new roots are well established. The stem can then be cut from the old plant and potted up in a shady place before planting it out in the garden two or three weeks later. If plants are divided or the rooted layerings dug up in the early spring, they can be planted directly into the ground.

Growing: Very easy care, once the plant is established. Old plants will benefit from a late winter top-dressing of finely sieved compost with a little dolomite lime added. Greek oregano is one of the herbs that maintain their flavor well on drying. Cut the stems as blossoming starts, tie into bundles, and hang up in a room to dry. When the bundles are dry, keep them in paper bags so they do not get dusty.

The tall oreganos can be vigorous spreaders and self-seeders. They are not as bad as mint but can overwhelm less vigorous herbs. The taller plants tend to flop over after flowering and need to be cut back during the winter to reveal the beautiful young leaves that appear in early March.

PARSLEY, CURLY *Petroselinum crispum*
PARSLEY, ITALIAN *P. c.* var. *neapolitum*

Both biennial or short-lived perennial

Italian parsley has flat, notched, dark green leaves. The flowering stem can be over 3 feet (90 cm) in height. Curly parsley has the familiar tightly curled leaflets associated with a parsley garnish.

Parsley, in addition to its use as the ever-present restaurant garnish, is used for flavoring. Italian parsley has a stronger taste and is preferred by many chefs for soups, meat dishes and stir-fries. It is also a delicacy when fried in a light tempura batter. Curly parsley is more ornamental.

Sun/Shade: Full sun to full shade. It has the best flavor in full sun, but is unlikely to set seed in full shade.

Soil: Best in rich, moist soil.

Hardiness: Listed as hardy to zone 2; both are hardy through most winters.

Pests/Diseases: None serious. Parsley is sometimes attacked by leaf miner, but the affected leaves can be removed without much damage to the plant.

Seeds: All the catalogs carry both types of parsley, though Richters has the widest selection.

Starting: It is best started from seed. In the early spring, soak the seed in wet paper towelling until a tiny, white root appears. Then sow the seed in a well-composted bed, sowing two or three seeds every 6 inches (15 cm) in rows 12 inches (30 cm) apart. If you buy plants, make sure that they are young seedlings and have not started to grow a flower stalk.

Growing: Very easy care. A month after planting in the ground, feed with fish fertilizer or top-dress the soil with compost. When cut heavily, the plant should be fed with nitrogen-rich fertilizer. If you are able to keep cutting out the flower stalks, the plants will keep on growing leaves for two or three years. Both curly and Italian parsley will self-seed if the seed heads are left to maturity. (See the celeriac entry for a description of chemicals in parsley that may cause temporary skin discoloration.)

PEA *Pisum sativum* Annual

There are three main types of peas: shelling, snap and snow. The snaps, like the snows, are eaten whole, but the pods are fatter, sweeter and juicier. The first picking of peas in May or June is one of the garden's sweetest moments.

Sun/Shade: Full sun is best.

Soil: Soils in the coastal Pacific Northwest are slightly acidic. It is help-ful to dig dolomite lime plus bone meal or rock phosphate into the soil the fall before sowing.

Hardiness: Hardy at Ravenhill. Overwintered peas survive two years out of three.

Pests/Diseases: Planting early types and germinating them in soil blocks are the two best methods of avoiding the fungal problems of cold soils. The enation virus, a summer problem, is reduced by using enation-resistant seed.

Seeds: Abundant Life, Nichols and Territorial have excellent selec-tions for the Pacific Northwest. Salt Spring carries several kinds of peas suitable for making soups.

Starting: At Ravenhill a routine has been established of sowing 'Little Marvel' (from Abundant Life) in November and again in March, and adding a row of snap peas in April. The March and April sowings are made in soil blocks and planted out when the first leaves are well developed. This method avoids poor germination caused by cold soils. Digging in compost before sowing provides a ready source of nitrogen and decreases the need for the legume inoculant recommended by some growers.

Growing: Very easy care once the supports are in place. November-sown peas come through in two years out of three but there are sometimes gaps, which are resown in late February or early March. The November sowing matures mid-May to early June. The March sowing is harvested late June and early July. The April sowing of snap peas matures in July. Chicken wire is used for support, though tree prunings also work well for dwarf types.

PENNYROYAL *Mentha pulegium* Perennial

Matlike, small, dark green leaves produce ten-inch-high (25-cm) light purple flower spikes in late summer. Like all the mints, it can be invasive, particularly in rich, moist soil.

Pennyroyal is reputed to be an effective insect and flea repellent. It has been used for many centuries to flavor meat and sauces. Many books caution against its culinary use by pregnant women.

Sun/Shade: Full sun to full shade.

Soil: Average garden soil.

Hardiness: Listed as hardy to zone 6 and is hardy at Ravenhill.

Pests/Diseases: None.

Seeds: Available from both Richters and Nichols; also in plant form.

Starting: It is probably easiest to buy a plant from a specialty nursery. If it is well rooted it can be divided when taking it out of the pot. It is best grown on the edge of a garden where it can slowly spread in dry, shady corners without becoming a problem for less vigorous plants. Having just dug up an invasive patch, I now intend to grow it in a tub.

Growing: Very easy care; survives neglect.

PEPPER, SWEET *Capsicum annuum* Perennial grown as an annual
Annual sweet peppers bear fruits that can be green, yellow, orange,
red or purple. The plants grow to 3 feet (.9 m) high and 18 inches
(45 cm) across with attractive dark green leaves and white flowers.

Peppers are an excellent source of vitamin C and have myriad
uses in the kitchen. They are also ornamental in the vegetable and
flower garden.

Sun/Shade: Full sun to quarter shade.

Soil: Rich, well drained.

Hardiness: Tender. Like melons, peppers need the protection of a
cold frame to fruit successfully.

Pests/Diseases: No problems yet.

Seeds: Widely available.

Starting: At Ravenhill, we buy seedlings in late April or early May.
They are planted 16 inches (40 cm) apart in a cold frame. Half a
spadeful of compost is dug in below the location of each plant. We
plant a mix of 'Gypsy' and 'California Wonder'. 'Gypsy' is an early-
maturing variety, with a thin skin that turns from pale yellow to
pale red as it matures. 'California Wonder' is thicker-skinned and
turns from dark green to dark red.

Growing: Easy care. The plants are watered every three days, because
the soil is light and drains fast. The plants are supported by string
stretched across the cold frame. The top of the frame is removed in
July. The fruits are sometimes ready in July, but they do not usually reach a red color and maximum sweetness until August. Harvesting continues to late October.

POTATO *Solanum tuberosum* Annual
The one vegetable I would not leave behind on a one-way trip to
a temperate desert island is the spud. Whether prepared as tender,
freshly minted morsels, mashed with garlic and butter, or baked
until the olive-oil-soaked skin is crisp, potatoes satisfy the appetite.

Sun/Shade: Full sun to one-quarter shade.

Soil: The potato is one of the few vegetables that likes an acidic soil, preferably with a pH below 6.0. The soil should be fairly rich and high in organic material.

Hardiness: Tubers overwinter in the ground, but the leaves are susceptible to frost.

Pests/Diseases: Flea beetles, which cut holes in leaves, were a severe problem when we started to grow potatoes. But for the past ten years damage has been minor and does not affect the storage life.

Tubers: Widely available.

Starting: The first potato leaves to appear in the garden are always those of tubers that were missed by the fork the previous summer. There must be a message in this, so in the last three years a few early potatoes have been planted in a cold frame in November. They grow quite well and are enjoyed greatly, but do not produce abundantly. Our crop of earlies is planted at the beginning of March, normally using 'Early Epicure'. The main crop follows in April or early May with the planting of 'Yukon Gold' and/or 'Red Pontiac' with a few 'Yellow Bananas'.

The rows are trenched and compost is forked in, sometimes with the addition of wilted comfrey leaves. The compost is covered with 1 inch (2.5 cm) of soil, then the potatoes are planted 12 inches (30 cm) apart and covered with 3 inches (7.5 cm) of soil. For the past three years I have used our own seed potatoes, which sprout in paper bags on the cool garage floor.

The crop that results is good but tends to be small: not many reach the size where one potato is enough for one person. The 1994 soil test results showed that the soil's pH is now close to 7.0, above the level that most writers suggest is good for growing potatoes. The largest potatoes grown here were in freshly broken meadow ground, which was certainly more acidic. Another theory is that small-sized potatoes may result from using seed potatoes with more than three shoots. Each shoot is, in effect, a separate new potato plant, and too many shoots leads to overcrowding, the growth of small potatoes, and the surfacing of potatoes that green in the sunlight.

This year I added some sawdust and next year will attempt to lower the pH of the potato bed with peat moss. I shall also try to increase size by rubbing off some of the sprouted shoots before planting. At harvest time, the yields and size from potatoes with three main stems will be compared with potatoes with five or more main stems.

Some people do not recommend using your own seed potatoes due to the possible spread of viruses.

Growing: The stems of the potato plants are hilled up with earth when they are about 6 inches (15 cm) high. Watering depends largely on the condition of your soil—if grown on the flat in slow-draining rich soil, then watering may only be important at the first flowering stage. If, as at Ravenhill, the spuds are grown in raised beds with fast-draining soil, then watering should be frequent enough so that growth is continuous—in our case every three days, and every other day when the flower buds start to form. In 1993 and 1994 a straw mulch was put on the bed in May to reduce the amount of watering. The mulched potatoes yielded more heavily than those that were not mulched.

The early crop potatoes are dug as soon as they are big enough to eat. The main crop is dug after the tops go brown. The potatoes are left on the soil surface for a few hours to dry and then stored in brown paper bags on the floor of an unheated garage adjoining the house. In January, to prepare the sprouting potatoes for March planting, they are separated and placed in a single layer in the bottom of paper bags with the top of the bag open to the light.

PUMPKIN *Cucurbita pepo* cultivars Annual

Two pumpkin plants in one cold frame grow enough to decorate the kitchen, fill pies, and provide a bright orange, nutritious vegetable for the dinner plates. The many tentacles of the plants sprawl out of the cold frame like an octopus.

Sun/Shade: Full sun is best.

Soil: Rich, moist soil.

Hardiness: Tender; can only be planted out in a cold frame or when the soil is really warm.

Pests/Diseases: Sow bugs attack young seedlings when first planted out in the cold frame. Use rotenone around the stem to prevent damage. Mildew attacks the plants in September, but by then the pumpkins are well developed.

Seeds: Seeds are widely available. 'Rouge D'Etampes', which we brought back from Paris about ten years ago, is a startling dark orange-red, heavily ribbed pumpkin—a real eye-catcher. Seeds of this cultivar are now available from Cook's Garden, Shepherd's and Territorial.

Starting: In April, seeds are started in peat pots, covered with clear plastic bags, and placed over a heating unit, at the same time as cucumber, melon and squash. The plastic bag is removed when the first leaves appear.

Growing: The plants are put out, two to a 36- by 40-inch (.9- by 1-m) cold frame in May; the soil of the cold frame is enriched by a shovelful of compost. A little rotenone is sprinkled on the soil around each stem to prevent sow bugs from chewing the leaf edges. The soil is kept moist and a top-dressing of compost and blood meal is put around the plants in early July, at which time the top of the cold frame is removed.

If your garden has a warm microclimate, you may be able to sow outside in late May or early June and not need the protection of a cold frame.

RADISH *Raphanus sativus* Annual or biennial

A popular salad ingredient, the ubiquitous round red radish is often the first vegetable planted by children. It's easy to grow and very rewarding, as its large seeds germinate quickly and soon provide an edible crop of peppery roots.

The large types include the daikon radish, which we grow at Ravenhill. A huge white- or black-skinned root, it can grow to more than 12 inches (30 cm) long and 4 inches (10 cm) wide. It can be eaten raw or cooked, and is widely used in Chinese and Japanese cuisines.

Sun/Shade: Full sun to half shade.

Soil: Rich and moist is best, but radishes will survive and produce hotter roots in average dry soil.

Hardiness: Hardy.

Pests/Diseases: The maggot of the cabbage fly can cause severe damage. If it's a problem, grow radishes under a floating row cover, which also prevents leaf damage from the flea beetle.

Seeds: Seeds for small radishes are widely available. Nichols has the best selection for daikon radishes.

Starting: Sow the small radishes in place in February in a cold frame, or outside in March. At Ravenhill, these radishes are grown only as a spring crop under Reemay. Daikon is grown as a fall and winter crop, and sown in place in late July or August under Reemay.

Growing: Radishes are very easy care, though enough moisture should be provided so that growth is vigorous and continuous. Harvesting can take place at any stage. If daikon radishes are left in the ground into December they can be protected by 6 inches (15 cm) of sawdust and harvested through January and February.

ROSEMARY *Rosmarinus officinalis* Evergreen shrub

Rosemary comes in various disguises. Upright forms grow to over 6 feet (1.8 m) in height if unclipped and in sheltered locations. Clipped plants have dense foliage and tend to bush out more, sometimes to a width of 6 feet (1.8 m). Prostrate forms, such as 'Santa Barbara', grow to 12 inches (30 cm) in height in containers and have a most attractive drooping habit. Flower color ranges from pale to dark blue, pink, purple and white. Flowering time is dependent on the coldness of the winter and normally occurs between March and late May.

Rosemary is intensely fragrant. It's widely used for flavoring meat dishes and pasta, and in marinades, barbecue sauces and baking. It's an excellent ornamental in the flower, herb or vegetable garden, especially when trimmed once a year in the early summer.

Sun/Shade: Its fragrance is best in full sun. Established plants can survive in three-quarters shade but do not flower.

Soil: Our best (most vigorous) plants have their roots in contact with concrete. They are also in very fast-draining soil. Plant rosemary near a concrete path, wall or house foundation, or mix dolomite lime into the soil below and around the planting hole.

Hardiness: Upright forms are almost fully hardy at Ravenhill, provided they are given lime and excellent drainage. Prostrate or creeping forms are not hardy here in zone 8 and need to be brought into the house or cold greenhouse in late October.

Pests/Diseases: Most casualties probably result from some form of root fungus. On average, we lose one plant per year out of a total of twenty-five plants, but we have one plant that has been in place for fifty years. The plants cannot stand poorly drained soil and need to get their roots well down into the subsoil. It is probable that the plant's susceptibility to root fungus is determined by the amount of moisture that remains around the roots in winter. In my experience, if a major branch of a rosemary plant turns brown and dies with no sign of a cut or break in that branch, then the rest of the plant will go the same way within a year or two. Cutting out the dead branch makes the plant look better, but does not appear to prolong the life of the rest of the bush. The dead plant should be burned.

Seeds: Nichols carries seeds and plants (both upright and creeping). Cook's Garden, Abundant Life and Territorial carry *Rosmarinus officinalis*. Richters carries *R. officinalis* seeds and a number of cultivars as plants.

Starting: It is best to buy plants. Cuttings need careful treatment and seeds are slow.

Growing: Easy care. If planted away from concrete, sprinkle the soil surface with dolomite lime every three years. At Ravenhill the plants get a light yearly dressing of compost in the early spring and their new growth is cut back for the chefs twice a year, which results in a dense, mounded bush. Plants are not cut back after the end of August and watering is suspended at the same time to allow any new growth to toughen up before the first frost.

Rosemary grows very well in containers and tolerates house temperatures better than most herbs. The plants rarely need root pruning or potting up to a larger-sized container. We have had one plant in the same 5-inch (12.5-cm) container for five years. The roots now fill the container and watering is a matter of little and often, especially when the plant is left in a sunny position. The leaves benefit from being sprayed with water once a week. The plant is fertilized by watering through a yearly top dressing of compost applied when the plant is set outside in April. At the same time, the plant's leaves are given a good wash with a mild detergent-water mixture.

SAGE, GARDEN *Salvia officinalis* Perennial
Garden sage grows to a height and width of 3 feet (.9 m), with gray leaves and pink-purple-blue flowers to 4 feet (1.2 m).

Its aromatic leaves are widely used to flavor meat dishes and the flowers are edible. The plant attracts bees, and is used for tea and medicinal purposes. It's an excellent ornamental bush in leaf and flower.

A relatively new cultivar, 'Holt's Mammoth', has a different flavor and form from garden sage. It forms a lower, denser and more spreading bush, and although its leaf color is similar, it does not flower. It spreads readily: roots develop where its branches touch the ground. One five-year-old plant at Ravenhill has a height of 2 feet (.6 m) and a spread of 7 feet (2.1 m). Its flavor is sweeter and not quite so pungent as garden sage. It should have as many or more culinary uses but it is not widely grown. The bush is an excellent ornamental throughout the year.

Sun/Shade: Full sun to half shade. It's most aromatic in full sun.

Soil: Average to poor garden soil. Sage is said to prefer alkaline soils, but grows well at Ravenhill in a pH of just below 7.0 (slightly alkaline). Add dolomite lime if your soil is acidic.

Hardiness: Garden sage is fully hardy here; listed as hardy to zone 3. 'Holt's Mammoth' is hardy at least to zone 8.

Pests/Diseases: None at Ravenhill.

Seeds: Seeds of garden sage are widely available and Richters carries the plants as well. 'Holt's Mammoth' does not set seed and is available in plant form from Nichols and Richters and specialty nurseries.

Starting: Sow seeds if available or start from plants. If you buy plants, you will harvest the leaves a year earlier than if you sow seeds. Summer cuttings root easily in damp sand in the shade. If your soil is acidic, add dolomite lime to the soil below the planting hole. Wood ash is a useful additive for increasing the pH, or alkalinity, but should be used in moderation. Young plants need watering every two or three days until they are established.

Growing: Very easy care. Mature plants are highly drought-resistant. Top-dress lightly with compost or leaf mold in the early spring. Add dolomite lime and bone meal or rock phosphate every three years. Garden sage self-seeds but not so vigorously as to become a problem.

SAGE, PINEAPPLE *Salvia elegans* Evergreen shrub
This attractive, green-leafed, upright, rangy shrub grows to 3 feet (.9 m) with flowers to 4 feet (1.2 m). Its bright scarlet flowers will brighten the garden in October and through to March if the winter is mild. Cutting back makes the plant bushy.

The leaves and flowers of pineapple sage are sweet and mild-flavored. They can be used in desserts and drinks and for decoration. It's a good ornamental, especially at the back of a low border.

Sun/Shade: Full sun to half shade.

Soil: Average garden soil.

Hardiness: Quite tender. In a well-drained, sheltered site, it is likely to be cut back to ground level by a temperature of 20°F (–6°C). The root system is hardy to at least 13°F (–10°C).

Pests/Diseases: The plant does not seem to be bothered by pests or disease.

Seeds: Plants available from Nichols and Richters.

Starting: Cuttings or plants. If possible, give it a site protected from the north or northeast wind.

Growing: Pineapple sage creates its own neurotic tension in the gardener. Will it or won't it appear in April? A plant that I thought was dead, but had not dug out, came up again after two winters, though it is possible that the plant had sent up a few unnoticed leaves. So far we have not lost a plant.

SALSIFY *Tragopogon porrifolius* Biennial
SCORZONERA *Scorzonera hispanica* Perennial

These plants are grouped together because their uses and cultivation are similar. Both have long, thin, almost cylindrical roots; white in the case of salsify, black-skinned in the case of scorzonera. They are grown at Ravenhill as winter vegetables. Their flavor bears a slight similarity to that of oysters, due to their high iron content. They are tasty braised, sautéed, deep-fried or baked with a white sauce. Both salsify and scorzonera are peeled and put into acidulated water before cooking to prevent browning.

Sun/Shade: Full sun to one-quarter shade.

Soil: Rich, deep garden soil. A foot (30 cm) of soil is adequate.

Hardiness: The plants are grown as annuals for fall and winter harvesting. Severe frosts will damage the roots, but this can be prevented in our area by applying a 4-inch (10-cm) layer of sawdust in November.

Pests/Diseases: None at Ravenhill. If there is a problem with root maggots, grow under a floating row cloth as a preventive measure.

Seeds: Both are available from Nichols and Richters. Abundant Life carries salsify.

Starting: Sow seed in May.

Growing: Very easy care. Harvesting can begin in September but the roots can be left in the ground over the winter. Digging them can be frustrating, as the roots are deep, and if you leave a fragment it will regrow.

SAVORY, SUMMER *Satureja hortensis* Annual

Summer savory grows on erect stems to 18 inches (45 cm) with narrow 1/2- to 1-inch-long (1.25- to 2.5-cm) leaves. Small pink flowers appear in July-August.

Known as the bean herb, the mildly peppery leaves are also used in many potato, egg and meat dishes.

Sun/Shade: Full sun to half shade. Flavor is strongest in full sun.

Soil: Average to rich garden soil.

Hardiness: Sow after the last frost and harvest in the summer and fall before the first frost.

Pests/Diseases: Resistant to pests and diseases.

Seeds: Available at Abundant Life, Nichols, Richters, Shepherd's and Territorial.

Starting: Summer savory is best grown from seed, as container-grown plants quickly go to seed when transplanted. Sow in April in a composted bed.

Growing: Very easy care. Plants should be thinned to 4 to 6 inches (10 to 15 cm) apart. Harvesting in small quantities can start when the plants are 8 inches (20 cm) high.

SAVORY, WINTER *Satureja montana* Evergreen shrublet

This fragrant, small, narrow-leafed, woody-stemmed bush grows to 12 inches (30 cm) in height and breadth. It bears small white flowers in July–August.

The leaves are somewhat similar in flavor to summer savory, but are stronger and more resinous and can be picked year round. It is excellent for flavoring bean dishes, as well as pork and beef. It makes a good ornamental for the rock garden or an informal hedge.

Sun/Shade: Full sun to half shade. It's most aromatic in full sun.

Soil: Well-drained average garden soil.

Hardiness: Hardy at Ravenhill; listed as hardy to zone 4.

Pests/Diseases: None at Ravenhill.

Seeds: Seeds are available from Abundant Life, Nichols and Richters. Plants are available from Richters and specialty nurseries.

Starting: Seeds, cuttings or layering.

Growing: Very easy care. Weekly watering may be necessary in dry weather, but when the plants are well established they need almost no water. The plants should be trimmed back in late winter and dead stems cut out. Our plants are given a yearly application of leaf mold.

SHALLOTS   *Allium cepa* (Aggregatum Group)   Perennial
Tubular onion-type leaves grow to 24 inches (60 cm) in height, occasionally with a white flower head. The most commonly grown bulbs are small, slightly elongated, purple shading to white with a brown cover when dry. The bulbs form clusters at or near the surface of the ground.

The bulbs are widely used as an onion with a delicate, sweet garlic flavor. Shallots are used in soups, stock and sauces, such as Béarnaise sauce, sprinkled on salads or chopped into vinegar and pickled whole.

Sun/Shade: Full sun is best, though small bulbs can be produced in half shade.

Soil: Rich garden soil which should be well drained.

Hardiness: Hardy at Ravenhill.

Pests/Diseases: None yet at Ravenhill.

Seeds: Normally grown from bulbs, which are available from Cook's Garden, Nichols and Richters. The same companies also carry the Dutch, or Atlantic, shallot, which is a high-yielding multiplier onion that lacks the delicate flavor and sweetness of the French shallot.

Starting: Buy bulbs, but beware the store-bought shallot. First, it may not be the true shallot. The French word "l'echalotte" is used for the Dutch multiplier onion. Second, the bulbs may have been treated with a growth inhibitor. I once bought some particularly fine French shallots from a grocery store and performed the usual rituals of bed preparation, planting, weeding and watering. The shallots did not respond. They sat there through December, January and February without a root hair or a leaf shoot. I dug them up in March and they were in the same fine condition as when I planted them in October. So buy your bulbs from the catalog or a nursery.

The bulbs can be planted in October or late February to early March. Prepare the bed by adding organic material, preferably compost. The bed should be well drained. If your drainage is poor, a raised bed may be necessary for October planting. The bulbs are planted root base down, 5 inches (12.5 cm) apart in rows 6 inches (15 cm) apart. I like to make a low planting ridge and set the bulbs in with their tops just showing at the soil surface.

Growing: October plantings should show some green by late December. In late February and two weeks later, fertilize with a nitrogen-rich fertilizer. Blood meal is an excellent, fast-acting source of nitrogen. Fish fertilizer is also good.

Keep the shallots well watered in any dry periods in March, April and early May. The watering and the nitrogen make strong and healthy leaves, which in turn grow large bulbs. Some gardeners add a phosphorus- and potassium-rich fertilizer in May to aid root growth. This is only important if you do not dig compost into the bed before planting.

In May it is a good idea to stop watering to allow the bulbs to mature for harvesting in July. When the leaves turn brown and fall over, the bulb clusters can be carefully forked up and the roots exposed to the sun for a day. The clusters should then be placed on racks in a warm, dry place until the tops and necks are completely dry (if you're braiding them, they should be braided before the tops are quite dry). When the tops are dry they can be cut off and the shallots stored in net bags in a cool, dark, dry, airy place.

SORREL, FRENCH *Rumex scutatus* Perennial

The broad, arrow-shaped, lush green leaves of sorrel grow to 8 inches (20 cm) in length. The fleshy, tubular flower spike rises to 2 feet (60 cm) if it escapes the scissors. Leaves stay green and usable through most winters. The plant spreads slowly.

The lemony leaves are used in soups, salads, sauces and fish dishes. The leaves are ornamental when the plant is grown in its own bed and the flower spike removed, but sorrel has little value in the flower garden.

Sun/Shade: Full sun to half shade. Best in full sun.

Soil: For tender leaves, the plant needs rich soil, well supplied with water and nitrogen. The site should drain quickly in the winter.

Hardiness: Hardy at Ravenhill; listed as hardy to zone 3.

Pests/Diseases: Leaf miner sometimes attacks individual leaves, which can be removed without harm to the plant.

Seeds: Available from most seed houses. Richters has the widest variety, with several kinds of culinary sorrel; one called 'Profusion', claimed to be seedless, is carried only as a plant.

Starting: Sow seed, or divide old plants in the late winter as growth starts. The site should be deeply dug and organic material added, as sorrel is a deep-rooted, long-lived plant. Space about 1 foot (30 cm) apart.

Growing: Water daily until the plants are well established. Established plants need little water or fertilizer unless they are being heavily cut. Ravenhill's sorrel gets a top-dressing of compost in late winter and again in June, and is given fish fertilizer every two weeks. Flower stalks should be removed as they form.

SPINACH *Spinacia oleracea* Annual or biennial

Spinach has broad, dark green leaves that are smooth or crinkled, depending on the type. Flower spikes rise to 3 feet (.9 m).

Spinach is an excellent year-round salad green, and can be cooked in soups and quiches or steamed.

Sun/Shade: Full sun to half shade.

Soil: Rich, moist, with good winter drainage.

Hardiness: Some kinds of spinach overwinter in zone 8.

Pests/Diseases: Leaf miner may be a summer problem. The damaged leaves can be picked off and destroyed.

Seeds: All the catalogs carry seeds for summer and winter growing.

Starting: It is important to choose a mildew-resistant kind of spinach if you are seeding in July or August for a fall, winter and early spring crop. For March through May seedings, choose a slow-bolting type.

After a number of germination and seedling failures I now always presoak the August seeding in damp paper towelling until the tiny root appears (three or four days). The March seeding is made into a tray of soil blocks covered with a clear plastic bag and placed over a heat source until the seedlings appear. The plastic bag is then removed and the tray placed in a cool greenhouse until the first leaves develop.

Growing: Spinach needs a lot of nitrogen and moisture. Add blood meal to the compost when preparing the ground. Feed with a nitrogen-rich fertilizer like fish fertilizer every two weeks when the plants are being cut. It is especially important to add nitrogen to the overwintered spinach in late February and early March when there is little nitrogen available to the plants from the soil.

TARRAGON, FRENCH *Artemisia dracunculus* 'Sativus' Perennial Narrow green leaves to 2 inches (5 cm) long grow on stems to 2 feet (60 cm) high. It has inconspicuous sterile flowers. The leaves have an intense, sweet, licorice flavor which is widely used in sauces, salads, vinegars, fish, chicken and egg dishes.

Russian tarragon (*A. dracunculus*) has larger leaves, sets seeds and has no culinary merit. Nurseries sometimes mislabel the plants, so check before you buy.

Sun/Shade: Full sun to half shade; the flavor is best in full sun.

Soil: Average to rich garden soil.

Hardiness: Completely hardy if the drainage is good; listed as hardy to zone 3.

Pests/Diseases: Spittlebugs are a minor problem; they do little damage and can be washed off with a hard water spray.

Seeds: Not available. Plants can be purchased from Nichols, Richters and Cook's Garden, as well as specialty nurseries.

Starting: Start by root division or summer cuttings. Old plants are very easy to divide in March or April when the first fresh green shoots appear. The old plant should be dug up and separated into 2- to 3-inch-long (5- to 7.5-cm) roots, each with a growing green shoot. These can then be potted up in shade for later planting in three weeks when the roots have started to grow again. It is possible to directly plant the root divisions, but they need careful watering and the soil should not be allowed to dry out. The initial site for the plant should be deeply dug with some added compost. If your soil suffers from slow winter drainage, then a raised bed is essential for survival of the plant.

Growing: Very easy care. Our beds get top-dressed with compost in the early spring when the dead tops are cut off. The plants are watered every three or four days and get a dose of fish fertilizer when they are heavily cut. Tarragon is quite drought-tolerant, but if it is neglected in a hot summer the leaves will turn brown. It can then be cut down to 6 inches (15 cm) above ground level, watered and later fertilized when new growth has started. Heavy cutting in September is not advised as it reduces the ability of the plant to get through the winter.

Our oldest tarragon bed is now showing some loss of flavor after seven years of growth. The roots have become a tangled mass and can no longer supply enough nutrients to produce the flavorful oils in the leaves.

Because of the size of the root system, tarragon is only good for a short time in a small pot. It needs at least a 2-gallon (9-L) container and even in this, the flavor of the leaves is likely to wane after two or three years.

THYMES *Thymus* spp. Perennial

There are more than one hundred kinds of thyme and naming is difficult because of the similar nature of some of them and the cross-pollination that occurs. The main culinary thyme grown at Ravenhill is lemon thyme (*T.* x *citriodorus*). Smaller quantities of French, or common English, thyme (*T. vulgaris*) and caraway thyme (*T. herba-barona*) are also grown.

The vibrant green growth of young lemon thyme plants in the spring is one of the delights of the herb garden. It is an evergreen that matures into a 12-inch-high (30-cm) plant with a similar spread. It carries small pink flowers in June to early July. The lower branches sometimes root and the plant grows slowly outward. After four or five years the foliage becomes thin and the woody stems are exposed.

The highly fragrant leaves of lemon thyme are used to flavor soups, sauces, marinades, meat and vegetable dishes. It attracts bees and makes a good tea. It is a pleasing ornamental in the vegetable, rock and flower garden and a good container plant.

Caraway thyme is a creeping, small-leafed evergreen. It has attractive pink flowers in June, but does not produce many leaves. The distinctive caraway flavor of the leaves adds zest to many meat dishes. It's an excellent ornamental ground cover in the rock garden and is used to attract bees and for herbal teas.

French, or common, thyme produces grayish, narrow, small leaves on an upright small shrub to 16 inches (40 cm) high and 24 inches (60 cm) wide. It has pink flowers in early June. Its culinary uses are similar to lemon thyme. It is an essential ingredient of herbes de Provence and bouquet garni.

Sun/Shade: Full sun to half shade. Caraway thyme can tolerate three-quarters shade. All grow best and are most fragrant in full sun.

Soil: Average garden soil with good winter drainage. Add dolomite lime if your soil is acidic.

Hardiness: Hardy at Ravenhill in well-drained sites. The common thyme is listed as hardy to zone 5; lemon thyme to zone 6; and caraway thyme to zone 3.

Pests/Diseases: None.

Seeds: Lemon thyme is only available as a plant; you can get it from Nichols and Richters and from specialty nurseries. Caraway thyme plants are available from Nichols and Richters. Common thyme seeds and plants are available from Nichols and Richters. Shepherd's and Abundant Life also carry seeds of common thyme.

Starting: Start lemon and caraway thyme from cuttings, layering or root division. Root division is especially easy and might even be called a form of layering if you mound up an established plant with sand or a sand and peat-moss mix, or even with light soil so that the lower branches are covered. The same effect can be achieved by digging up an entire plant in March (after thoroughly watering it) and replacing it in a hole that is 4 inches (10 cm) deeper, which buries all the lower branches. Both these methods should result in rooted branches four weeks later. These can then be cut off, potted up and grown in the shade for three weeks before planting out in the garden. When the plantlets are being potted up, shorten the leafy growth by three-quarters. Cuttings taken in late spring root readily in damp sand in the shade. Cut off about 3 inches (7.5 cm) of new growth, remove the lower leaves, and push the stem into the sand. Cuttings should be kept in the shade until they are well rooted and show some new growth. Common thyme can be started from seed, from bought plants or by taking cuttings. Layering or root division is difficult because of the single-stemmed upright form of the plant.

Growing: The thymes are very easy care. They are drought-tolerant, but produce few new leaves after the spring if kept dry. Plants grown quickly in rich soil look better but probably have less of the aromatic oils that contain the flavors. The plants get a sprinkling of dolomite lime with some rock phosphate every three years. In late February or early March I try to give them a spring tonic of liquid fish fertilizer. Harvesting can take place every month of the year but should not be heavy after the end of August. Older plants should be cut back in the late winter.

Lemon thyme makes an attractive container plant for two or three years, but does not care for normal winter house temperatures. It overwinters well in a cool greenhouse or cold frame, or under the house eaves.

TOMATO *Lycopersicon esculentum* Perennial grown as an annual

The bewildering array of tomatoes available makes it difficult to choose the right one to grow. Color ranges from yellow through red to purple, and size, sweetness and acidity vary. Then there is a choice between bush/determinate and staking/indeterminate types. Bush take up more space but need less labor. Staking take less space but must be tied to a stake or string.

The main challenge for the coastal gardener is to grow a fully vine-ripened tomato in a climate where cool nights slow the warming of the soil.

Some gardens have excellent microclimates and fruit will ripen on the vine without artificial aids. It is a good idea to choose early-ripening tomatoes, especially those that have been bred or proven under coastal conditions. But even then, many coastal gardens will benefit from some form of shelter. Shelter increases the heat around the plant, partly by reducing air circulation and partly, if the shelter has a cover, through the greenhouse effect by which energy enters easily but can only leave slowly. There is a trade-off here, however: the less air circulation, the earlier the ripening, but the greater the chance of fungal diseases.

The tomatoes carefully bred for yield, early maturity, disease resistance and keeping qualities are sometimes those with the least flavor. Flavor is determined partly by genetics and partly by the environment, and it is also a subjective matter determined by the individual taster. The sweetness component seems to be mainly controlled by the amount of sunlight, with an assist from the nutrients absorbed by the roots. My wife Noël's unscientific observation, based on her taste buds, is that home-compost-grown vine-ripened tomatoes are really the fruit that could not be resisted in the first garden. My theory is that Eve was tired of weeding and the forbidden fruit was just an excuse.

Sun/Shade: Full sun is best.

Soil: The soil should be rich and well supplied with potash.

Pests/Diseases: The possible diseases are almost as many as the number of cultivars. Blossom end rot is said to be a combination of irregular watering and calcium deficiency; it has not been a problem at Ravenhill since we started using our home compost ten years ago. Other diseases that affect the leaves seem to occur late in August and have not greatly reduced the productivity of the plants. Preventive disease measures include making sure there is good air circulation, not watering the leaves, growing the plants strongly without check, and rotating the plantings so that members of the same family—tomatoes, potatoes, eggplant and peppers—are not put in the same beds more than one year in three. In areas where late blight is a serious problem, experienced gardeners recommend the use of a copper-based fungicidal spray when the plants are young. If tomatoes have been infected, tomato stakes should be disinfected before reusing.

Seeds: Seeds are available from all catalogs except Richters, but those in the Territorial Seeds and Abundant Life catalogs are tested for coastal conditions.

Starting: A good selection of plants is available from nurseries in spring and we rarely grow from seed. In early April we buy plants that are about 6 inches (15 cm) tall and immediately pot them up into 6-inch-wide (15-cm) pots in a rich mix of soil and compost. The plants are put in a bright window with a minimum night temperature of 50°F (10°C). At the end of April, the plants are put out in the garden inside an open-topped plastic-sided frame 30 inches (75 cm) tall. Each planting hole is spaced 30 inches (75 cm) apart and prepared by digging in a shovelful of compost. We make the hole 12 inches (30 cm) deep; the lower part of the stem is stripped of leaves and buried, leaving about 6 inches (15 cm) of leafy stem above the ground.

Growing: Water every three days in dry weather. I always try to leave a watering depression around the stem of each plant, both to hold the early June top-dressing of compost and to direct the water toward the roots. Watering is by wand to avoid getting water on the leaves. The staking tomatoes are tied to 5-foot (1.5-m) stakes. The bush types are left to sprawl. After each plant has set five sprays of fruit, the new flowering shoots are removed.

This growing method matures early crop 'Oregon Spring' and 'Sweet 100' tomatoes in July, with the main crop—'Fantastic' and 'Alicante'—maturing in August. There has yet to be a large crop of green tomatoes. One hardy type, probably a yellow 'Currant' or similar cultivar, seeds itself and ripens its tiny fruits in September each year.

VERBENA, LEMON *Aloysia triphylla* (syn. *Lippia citriodora*) Shrub Lemon verbena has narrow, pale green leaves and will grow to be a 5-foot (1.5-m) shrub in a very warm, protected position. At Ravenhill it struggles up to 1 foot (30 cm) each year. It makes a good container plant.

It has a strong lemon flavor that is especially good for desserts, such as pound cake and custards, as well as fish and meat dishes and teas. It can also be an ingredient in potpourri.

Sun/Shade: Full sun to half shade.
Soil: Average garden soil.

Hardiness: Tender. The roots are hardy to at least 13°F (–10°C) in a well-drained but exposed site at Ravenhill. It is listed as hardy in zone 8, but I'm sure that the choice of site is critical to survival within this zone.

Pests/Diseases: None.

Seeds: Richters carries it as a plant; it is not available as seed from the catalogs listed here.

Starting: Buy a plant from Richters or a specialty nursery.

Growing: It is not an easy plant in the garden. We have kept plants growing outside for six years, but they are cut back to the ground each year by winter frosts and then struggle to send out new shoots in the late spring.

Our container plant does well; it is in a cool greenhouse from October to April and outside the rest of the year. We cut it back in the spring and give it a top-dressing of compost as soon as the new growth starts. Leaves can be harvested at any time.

II

THE
GROWING
ENVIRONMENT

SOIL ENRICHMENT

Of all the influences on the growth of plants, the soil is one of the most important, and while it can be modified by various additives, its complexity is so great that the effects of the additives are only partly understood.

As every site has its own microclimates and every plant has its own requirements for best growth, so every garden has its own soil characteristics. These characteristics must be understood so that the gardener can determine what plants are likely to do well, what changes can be made to the soil to make plants grow better, and whether the appropriate changes can be made to allow growing of some particular culinary treasure.

The starting point for understanding the soil, for the beginning gardener, is a soil test. The first and easiest is the pH test that determines the acidity/alkalinity balance of the soil. The optimum range for most vegetables and culinary herbs is between 6.5 and 7.2; neutral is 7.0.

Soils in the coastal region have a low pH (they are acidic), especially where the soil overlies granite or where it is high in organic material, such as from a forest floor, a bog, or a former lake bed.

The second test is for the amount of nitrogen (N), phosphorus (P) and potassium (K) available to the plants. These are essential nutrients. In coastal soils, potassium is usually high, but nitrogen and phosphorus are inadequate for the intensive cultivation of vegetables and some culinary herbs.

A third test is for the organic matter in the soil. The amount of organic material helps to determine the number of microorganisms as well as the amount of nitrogen that can be made available to the plant. If the amount of organic matter is high enough—about 5 percent—it enables the plants to take up phosphorus and potassium, which would otherwise not be available. Sandy and clay soils can be greatly improved with the addition of organic material. Soils high in organic matter warm up quickly in the spring, hold moisture well and, in general, provide an excellent medium for plant growth and health.

A more complete soil test includes magnesium, calcium, sodium, sulfur and the trace minerals iron, copper, boron, manganese and zinc. Deficiencies of these, with the exception of sodium, could cause growth problems. Sodium and boron cause problems if present in too large quantities.

The least complicated way of growing herbs and vegetables in the coastal areas of the Pacific Northwest is to make some assumptions about average soil conditions. Average soils are too acidic for optimum growth of most culinary herbs and vegetables, and they are too low in nitrogen and phosphorus. The simple answer is to add agricultural lime to those beds that are appropriate in the fall and to use dolomite lime in spot applications; mix the lime in well with the soil. Add compost and use green manures to maintain or increase the level of organic matter, and add nitrogen at critical times in each plant's life. Incorporate rock phosphate every three years in the fall to maintain adequate phosphorus levels. Trace element levels can be maintained by the use of compost and fish fertilizer and by maintaining the organic matter of the soil at a high level.

Soil Testing at Ravenhill

We had the soil tested for pH, nitrogen (N), phosphorus (P) and potassium (K) when we arrived in 1979. Nitrogen and phosphorus levels were low, potassium was quite high, and the pH was close to 6.0.

Since then the primary fertilizer has been compost made from garden waste, plus straw mixed with chicken and sheep manure. Blood meal and alfalfa are normally added to the compost. In the past, rock phosphate and wood ash have been added occasionally. In addition, two large loads of cow manure have been spread and dug in, in the fall. Most beds have had a winter green manure cover for the past seven years. The beds have had a scattering of rock phosphate on two occasions and agricultural lime three times.

Soil samples were taken in late February 1994 from ten different places in the vegetable garden from a depth of 6 inches (15 cm). Samples were also taken from the previous summer's covered compost piles and covered leaf mold that was sixteen months old.

	SOIL		COMPOST		LEAF MOLD		SUFFICIENCY RANGE FOR VEGETABLES
Organic matter	12.6%	H+	31.4%	VH	39.2%	VH	
pH	7.2	M+	7.4	M+	6.6	M+	5.5 to 7.5
Nitrate (N)	16 ppm	L	1088 ppm	VH	160 ppm	VH	30–50 ppm
Phosphorus (P)	573 ppm	VH	1251 ppm	VH	136 ppm	H	75 ppm
Potassium (K)	511 ppm	VH	7030 ppm	VH	469 ppm	H	175 ppm
Magnesium	453 ppm	VH	1096 ppm	VH	340 ppm	VH	
Calcium	3124 ppm	VH	3414 ppm	VH	2491 ppm	VH	
Sodium	70 ppm	M	478 ppm	VH	48 ppm	VL	
Sulphate	45 ppm	VH	361 ppm	VH	32 ppm	VH	
Boron	1.9 ppm	VH	6.03 ppm	VH	5.08 ppm	VH	
Copper	2.0 ppm	H	1.7 ppm	H	1.2 ppm	H	
Iron	91.6 ppm	VH	49.9 ppm	VH	24.9 ppm	H	
Manganese	16.5 ppm	VH	19.4 ppm	VH	28.2 ppm	VH	
Zinc	27 ppm	VH	28.9 ppm	VH	31 ppm	VH	

ppm = parts per million   VH = very high   H = high   M = medium   L = low   VL = very low

Each reading in parts per million is the amount available to the plant; 10,000 ppm = 1 percent. Each category is rated by the lab as to its sufficiency for growing an average crop. The sufficiency ranges of N, P and K are for field crops and should be increased for intensive garden growing.

SOIL TEST RESULTS

The percentage and type of organic matter is an important guide to the health of the soil and its ability to provide plants with nitrogen. If the organic matter is in the form of unbroken-down plant material (for example, fresh sawdust or straw), the bacterial action will reduce the level of nitrogen available to plants. If the organic matter has already been broken down in compost-making or exposure to the soil, the bacteria colonizing it will make more nitrogen available to the plant.

At 7.2, the pH of the soil at Ravenhill is higher (more alkaline) than the optimum for growing potatoes, but it is within the best range for most vegetables and culinary herbs. The addition of dolomite lime and wood ash over fifteen years has probably caused the increase from a pH of 6.0 in 1980. The alkalinity of the compost (7.4) has also played a role. The message from this is not to add dolomite or wood ash for a few years and to add peat moss or leaf mold to the next potato bed.

Our test results show that the available nitrogen levels in the soil are low. It would have been interesting to know what the nitrate level was in the same beds in early October to find out how much nitrogen was lost to the winter rains. The low nitrate level stresses the importance of adding nitrogen-rich fertilizer (compost, fish fertilizer or blood meal) to overwintering plants, as growth starts in late winter. Examples include shallots, garlic, chives, kale, spinach, broccoli, arugula, cress, corn salad and parsley. For that matter, the perennial culinary herbs also benefit from an early spring nitrogen tonic.

The amount of available nitrogen necessary to grow plants varies from between 20 and 30 parts per million for most perennials and between 30 and 50 ppm for vegetables under field conditions. Salad greens, basil, sorrel, spinach, squash and corn are all heavy nitrogen users, and high-nitrogen compost is an essential ingredient for growing these plants. If strong compost is not available, satisfactory alternatives are blood meal, canola seed meal and fish fertilizer.

The phosphorus level is seven times the sufficiency level for vegetables and perennials and the potassium is almost three times the sufficiency level. Neither level is enough to harm crops, but there is certainly no need to add rock phosphate for a few years.

Overall, testing of the soil, compost and leaf mold has shown that the soil enrichment methods at Ravenhill are providing the necessary organic matter, nutrients and trace elements for the intensive growth of vegetables and culinary herbs. This theoretical conclusion reinforces the practical observation that most of the plants grow very well.

The keys to the enrichment process are the use of compost and green manures to maintain organic matter, plus the use of additives to increase the nitrogen, phosphorus and trace element levels of both the compost and the soil to suit the special demands of the plants.

Compost

It is almost impossible to overestimate the benefits of using compost in the garden. Compost adds organic matter to the soil, as well as available nitrogen (N), phosphorus (P), potassium (K) and trace elements. It improves the water-holding ability of the soil and thereby reduces the amount of watering. It improves the crumb structure of the soil, and makes locked-up nutrients available. It can be used to change the pH of the soil. Because plants grow well with compost, it reduces insect damage and the use of insecticides. Compost makes your vegetables and herbs taste as though they came from the Garden of Eden!

Are there any disadvantages to using compost? There are some cautions: the strong compost at Ravenhill can harm some plants if added undiluted close to the plant roots; and careless composting may attract rats and spread weed seeds and plant diseases.

At Ravenhill, the compost piles provide almost all the nutrients for the vegetables and for the leafy herbs that require a rich soil. The richness of the compost is supplied by additives, such as sheep manure, chicken manure, blood meal and occasionally horse manure, which are included when we make the pile.

The compost plays an important role in every aspect of the garden. It is mixed with leaf mold and soil for potting up container plants. Compost is dug into new beds for basil, potatoes, tomatoes, onions, lettuce, spinach, celeriac, squash, corn and all the heavy feeders before sowing or planting out; the heaviest feeders get an additional thin layer of compost around their stems in July. Perennial herbs, like sorrel, chives and tarragon, are given a top-dressing of compost in the early spring as growth starts and again in July. Large container plants are given a top-dressing at the same time. The mixed shrub, flower and herb border is top-dressed with a mix of compost and leaf mold in late February or early March. Acid lovers get leaf mold.

Home gardeners with access to kitchen and garden wastes can make excellent compost using additives, such as blood and bone meal, available from garden centers.

THE COMPOST SOIL TEST

A look at the chart reveals that Ravenhill's compost is high in organic matter and that the nitrogen, phosphorus and potassium content, as well as the trace elements, are well over sufficiency levels. There is a very high boron count; three times the maximum level recommended for some vegetable and soft fruit crops. If this level were present in the garden soil, it would be a problem, but because the compost is always diluted with soil it is most unlikely to cause any damage.

The pH level of 7.4 is getting to the high end of the range within which most vegetables flourish. The level can be reduced by not adding dolomite lime or wood ash to the compost.

MAKING COMPOST: METHOD 1—COLD COMPOSTING

There are two ways to make compost: the hot method and the cold method. The latter is more appropriate for urban gardeners as the hot method is more dependent on the use of manure, large containers and frequent turning.

Use two parts green material—unsprayed grass clippings, green plant material, and vegetable and fruit kitchen waste—to one part brown material—dry leaves, sawdust (in small amounts), and chopped or shredded woody stems. Avoid weed seeds and diseased material.

Alternate the layers of green and brown material. To each brown layer, add a shovelful of garden soil and a handful each of blood and/or bone meal and dolomite lime. Sprinkle the layer with water, adding enough to dampen the pile, but not so much that it leaks out or pools in the bottom of the container.

In urban areas the compost container should be a rat-proof mesh, metal or heavy plastic container. Mesh containers should be covered with plastic to prevent rain leaching out nutrients. The compost will be ready in four to six months. Turning the pile is not essential, but it does speed up the process of decomposition.

MAKING COMPOST: METHOD 2—HOT COMPOSTING

This method is appropriate for gardeners who have access to rural material and who relish the challenge and effort involved.

Use two parts green material—unsprayed grass or hay, green plant material, vegetable and fruit kitchen waste, and alfalfa—to one part brown material—dry leaves, sawdust (not more than 10 percent of the total), straw, chopped or shredded woody stems, and chicken and/or sheep manure, preferably straw-based.

Gather enough material to make a pile at least 1 cubic yard (.9 m) in size. This is close to the minimum size for a hot compost pile. Grass and hay should be used shortly after cutting as they decompose rapidly, so at Ravenhill compost-making is usually planned for a grass-cutting day.

The ingredients are added in 3- to 6-inch (7.5- to 15-cm) layers, alternating green (nitrogen-rich) and brown (carbon-rich) layers. Sprinkle each layer with a shovelful of soil, a handful each of dolomite lime, wood ash, blood meal and bone meal (omit the dolomite if the pH of the soil is above 7.0). The pile is moistened as it is built, but not so much that water leaks from the base of the pile. The pile is then covered with black plastic to retain moisture and heat and prevent rain from leaching out nutrients. If the mixture of carbon and nitrogen-rich material is roughly right, the pile should heat up to about 150°F (63°C) within two days.

Four or five days after making the pile it should be turned with a fork. This provides oxygen and moves the outer, less composted material to the center of the pile.

In another four days it can be turned into a storage bin; it is ready to use after ten days, when it has cooled down. If the pile does not heat up strongly, it is left in covered storage for at least three months, in which time the worms work their alchemy on the compost. During the May to August period the hot method is reliable; in April and September the cooler air decreases the chance of making a hot pile.

It is a good idea to fill a storage bin by October; it can then be applied to the soil in March, April and May. The storage bin is also useful as a place to dig in kitchen waste during the winter months. The worms quickly break down kitchen scraps.

Oxygen is vital to decomposition, and there are two methods of getting more oxygen to the center of the pile. When your pile is about 18 inches (45 cm) high, push a 4- to 5-foot (1.2- to 1.5-m) stake vertically down through the center of the pile, then go on layering the pile around the stake. Wiggle the stake so that it slightly compresses the sides of the hole, remove the stake and cover the pile with black plastic. Every day, remove the plastic, insert the stake and wiggle it around for a minute or two. Another way of getting more oxygen is to build your pile on three rows of bricks covered crosswise with twigs. This structure allows air to circulate up from beneath the pile. Both these methods work well, but the outer parts of the pile will still not be composted without turning the pile once. Another approach is to put the less composted material in a storage bin for later addition to a new pile.

At Ravenhill there are six compost bins, one of which is usually reserved for piling ingredients, two for two stages of new compost, and two or three for storage. The bins are made from untreated rough cedar and are big enough to make a pile in one side and then turn it into the other side of the same box. Each bin is 6 feet (1.8 m) long, 4 feet (1.2 m) wide and 3 feet (.9 m) high with a 3-foot-wide (.9-m) opening. The corner posts rest partly on concrete, partly on earth. After thirteen years, the bottom parts of the boxes are starting to rot out but are still serviceable. The boxes are not rat-proof, but care is taken not to put in any meat or dairy products.

SHREDDING

Shredding stalky and twiggy material makes a big difference to composting. It exposes a much larger volume of the plant to bacterial action and greatly increases the speed of decomposition and the chances of making a hot pile.

At Ravenhill we have used an electric shredder for seven years. It is great for dry, stalky material like raspberry and blackberry canes, fennel stalks, tarragon stalks, asparagus ferns, old peonies and corn stalks. However, the machine cannot handle moist, soft material, it cannot take in dry leaves quickly enough, and it cannot cope with a lot of crooked twigs or twigs larger than about 1/2 inch (1.25 cm) in diameter. There are powerful gas-driven drum-type shredders with attached chippers, but of course these are more costly and mechanically complicated. It is also possible to rent a commercial machine for the two or three times a year that it's used.

Leaf Mold

Leaf mold is a primary source of organic material and slow-release fertilizer for the mixed herb, flower and shrub beds. Any that is left over is used in making potting soil or occasionally put on the vegetable garden.

The soil test of sixteen-month-old covered leaf mold (see page 97) showed high organic content and nitrate levels (five to seven times that sufficient for perennials). Phosphorus, potassium and trace element levels are all sufficient for growth.

The leaves are collected mainly from oaks, maples and copper beeches and are placed in an 8- by 12-foot (2.4- by 3.6-m) wire-netting bin in late October and November. The leaves are watered, sometimes a little blood meal is added to aid decomposition and provide an added boost for the plants, and the bin is covered with black plastic until the following October. The black plastic retains moisture, helps speed decomposition, keeps wind-blown seeds from getting into the wrong place, and prevents winter rains from washing out the nitrogen in the blood meal. In October the leaf mold is shovelled into plastic garbage bags and stored outside until late February or March, when it is distributed around the garden.

A small, separate bin is reserved for leaves which are slow to break down, like those of the English laurel. Every three years or so the laurel leaves are added to the main bin.

Mechanical shredding of the leaves would certainly greatly speed up decomposition of the leaf mold; it could then be used the following spring, rather than one year later.

Supplemental Fertilizers

Application of supplemental fertilizers varies according to the plant, the deficiencies of your soil, the time of year and the availability of compost. For example, potatoes and tomatoes are heavy users of potassium, and tomatoes also need calcium to prevent blossom end rot. Potatoes grow better with a slightly acidic soil (low calcium). Tomatoes need supplemental feeding as fruit forms in June and July. Potatoes demand less nitrogen and they are not given additional fertilizer after planting.

Supplements used at Ravenhill include agricultural lime and dolomite lime (which contains magnesium as well as lime), fish fertilizer, canola seed meal, liquid seaweed, wood ash, rock phosphate, bone meal and blood meal. A few years ago we were also using a fair amount of mushroom compost as a top-dressing and soil improver. Since then we have increased the amount of compost we make and stopped adding mushroom compost when the local supplier closed down.

In fifteen years we have brought in two small loads of horse manure and three truckloads of aged cow manure. The horse manure is bought in late spring and is all composted to get rid of the undigested weed seeds. The cow manure is spread in the fall before sowing the fall rye. The winter rain removes any soluble nitrogen not taken up by the rye, but the manure is an excellent soil conditioner.

Green Manures

This term refers to the practice of planting cover crops to maintain or increase the productive capacity of the topsoil.

Green manures can be used to increase the organic content of soil, increase its nitrogen content and the amount of other nutrients and trace elements, and improve the looseness and ease of cultivation of the soil. They also protect it from the dust-bowl effects of summer and the leaching out of soluble nutrients by winter rains. In addition, green manures prevent the disintegration of the crumb structure of the top-soil. Green manures can be valuable as a source of compost material and food for the kitchen.

At Ravenhill, the green manure we use most frequently is winter rye, but we have also sown Austrian field pea, hairy vetch and buck-wheat. Seeds for all these are normally available in bulk from feed stores or large garden centers.

One of the most useful characteristics of winter rye is that if for rea-sons of laziness, distractions or absence you didn't get the fall cleanup done until November, there is still time to sow the winter rye. It can be sown any time up to first frost, which is usually around mid-November in our area. I have sown it with success in the first week of December, but wouldn't like to take the chance again.·

Winter rye is a great producer of root mass, and thus of organic material which remains in the ground. It also acts as a weed suppres-sant and protects the soil from winter rain damage. If your soil has lit-tle organic matter or has been deprived of nutrients for years, it is a good idea to dig in animal manure or compost before sowing.

Before sowing the rye, prepare the bed by removing stones and using a rake to break up clumps of soil. Scatter the seeds by hand so that seeds are roughly 2 inches (5 cm) apart. Rake lightly to cover most of the seeds and keep the bed moist until germination.

If you have a problem with birds eating seed in your garden, try sowing in rows 6 or 8 inches (15 or 20 cm) apart and covering all the seed. If you have a serious bird problem—like thirty California quail choosing your newly sown bed as a fast-food outlet while dust-bathing—one option is to temporarily cover the bed with wire net-ting. This method also eliminates cat excavations.

Depending on when you dig or till the rye in, it can produce sub-stantial leaf growth. I prefer to dig it in before the tops grow over 10 inches (25 cm) high. The time for this depends on the soil tem-perature during winter. At Ravenhill we usually turn it under in late February or early March from an October sowing. Because we have raised beds and do not use a mechanical tiller, we dig it in with a shovel. Ideally, each spadeful should be inverted so that the leaves do not show above the ground. If leaves are left showing they will have to be pulled or hoed to prevent regrowth. Two or three passes with a tiller should result in turning all the grass under.

If the leaves have grown so tall that digging them under proves too difficult, cut the top growth for compost and turn the stubble under. The bed can be resown or planted two to three weeks after the rye is dug under. I have not used rye in the summer, but it is said to be excellent for suppressing weeds and for bringing poor land back into cultivation.

Hairy vetch and Austrian field pea are legumes and therefore help to fix nitrogen in the soil. Hairy vetch dies during the winter and the Austrian field pea is very easy to dig under in the spring. They have little root mass and are a good choice if your soil is already high in organic material. Using them reduces the amount of nitrogen that needs to be applied in the spring, but they should be sown in early September, about nine weeks before the first frost.

Buckwheat is an excellent summer green manure. It is deep-rooted, which brings up nutrients from the subsoil. It is drought-tolerant after the seedlings are established, but it has little in the way of root mass. Spring or early summer sowings of buckwheat should be dug or tilled under, or the tops composted, before seeds develop. Buckwheat winter-kills at the first frost and should be sown before the first week in September in our area. Late-summer sowings of buckwheat are sometimes combined with hairy vetch and Austrian field pea to provide continuous soil protection through the winter.

There are a number of winter green manures that appear to work well and also provide greens for the kitchen. Spring sowings of red Siberian kale, red Japanese mustard, mizuna, land cress and arugula, if allowed to flower, distribute their seeds to germinate in September or October. The hardy seedlings from these accidental sowings have survived the last two winters at Ravenhill (land cress for eight years) and make edible ground covers. They do not develop the extensive root mass of winter rye, but they are easy to pull out in the spring. Another edible green, corn salad (mache), has some potential as a winter green manure but needs to be sown before the end of August. The seeds of these edible ground covers are not normally available in bulk, unlike those of winter rye, buckwheat, Austrian field pea and hairy vetch. Thus, anything more than a small planting may be dependent on the gardener collecting his or her own seeds. The edible green manures do not have the capacity of winter rye for easy germination and growth in the cold soil of mid-October or later.

Winter rye is by far the most useful green manure that has been grown at Ravenhill.

WATER AND MULCH

Supplying the garden with water is one of the major concerns of all gardeners. Soil porosity (the amount of water the soil can hold) and soil permeability (the drainage, or speed with which water passes through the soil), weather, water supplies and the particular requirements of individual plants all determine how often and how long the garden is watered. I like to imagine that the fine feeder root hairs near the surface need the water the most and that they should have enough to be thoroughly damped, with enough to penetrate to the deeper roots in the subsoil. Too much water at one time washes soluble nutrients out of the topsoil and away from the feeder roots.

At Ravenhill, water is in short supply from a dry June to a dry October. There is enough for two families and a reasonable-sized garden, but not enough to expand the herb and vegetable growing area. The topsoil at Ravenhill is thin—6 to 9 inches (15 to 23 cm)—even in the raised beds, and it drains very quickly. A thicker topsoil with more clay would need less frequent watering. The amount of organic matter in the soil greatly affects the ability of the soil to hold moisture.

Watering is all done with a series of hoses and hand-held wands, and can take up to an hour and a half a day. The hose and wand system has maximum flexibility, uses very little water, and helps the gardener to observe the growth and problems of individual plants.

Other than arranging for rain to occur every third night, any watering method has its problems. Watering at Ravenhill takes a lot of time, but it is an activity that has its own rewards. We water in the early morning when the low sun casts defining shadows, the dew sparkles on the grass and the colors are intense—a good time for contemplation. On a less mystical level, it involves dragging unwieldy rubber hoses. Hose-dragging, which is due to be an Olympic sport in the twenty-second century, is made easier by placing 18-inch (45-cm) lengths of rebar in appropriate places throughout the garden and slipping white plastic pipe over the rebar so that the hose can negotiate corners without destroying plants in adjacent beds.

Sooner or later, most gardeners at least contemplate installing an automated watering system. It certainly reduces the labor component, but there are a few negative aspects. Automation is expensive, and it imposes a structure that reduces flexibility in planting. Overhead sprinkling, in particular, wastes a lot of water and does not cater to the individual needs of plants in complex beds.

There is also the problem of maintenance: at one time there was a capillary system for the apple orchard on the farm, but the black plastic pipes at the surface started to break down after ten years of summer sunshine and the rabbits chewed the capillary tubes.

Summer Mulch and Water Conservation

Summer mulches are both a method of water conservation and a way of maintaining the health and level of organic material in the soil.

In the winter, rain passes down through the saturated soil and subsoil, out to streams, lakes or the ocean. In the spring, the amounts of rain briefly balance the amount of moisture lost by evaporation and there is a little upward movement of soil moisture. By late spring, the amount of evaporation usually starts to exceed that of rainfall, and the soil and subsoil start to lose their winter charge of moisture. Mulch cannot prevent the loss of moisture downward, but it greatly reduces evaporation at the soil surface. Summer mulching also keeps the soil cool, encouraging the growth of shallow feeder roots and increasing the activity of microorganisms at the soil surface. In this way mulching is a form of slow composting, sometimes called sheet composting.

At Ravenhill, straw mulch is mainly applied in May as the soil starts to dry. It is placed around artichokes, fennel, raspberries, strawberries and tomatoes, and sometimes potatoes. I always mean to apply more straw to more plants and even to the paths between the beds, but there are so many jobs to do in May that the moment passes.

Mulching—A Case History

Sandra Holloway gardens a few miles from Ravenhill Herb Farm, and she has been applying thick straw mulch on one part of her garden and thick wood chips on a second part every year for more than a dozen years. The results show the great benefits that come from mulching.

Before mulching, the topsoil was a heavy, flat-lying clay. The original purpose of the mulch was to improve the soil with a minimum of labor. For twelve winters, 100 bales of straw were applied to 4,000 square feet (370 square m) and a 6-inch-thick (15-cm) layer of wood chips to another 2,000 square feet (185 square m) of garden.

On several occasions, the garden was rototilled just before applying the mulch, but this did not seem to make any difference to the vegetables. Weeds were a major problem for the first two years, but are now easily removed in a few minutes each week.

Nitrogen, in the form of urea, is added in the late winter at a rate of 26 pounds (12 kg) for 2,000 square feet (185 square m). This technically disqualifies the garden from being organic. However, it does seem to be true that there is a relationship between the harm done to the soil by inorganic nitrogen fertilizers and the amount of organic material in the soil. The greater the organic matter, the higher the dose of inorganic fertilizer the soil can tolerate. The thick mulch should also help in preventing soluble nitrates from reaching the water table. Organic growers can substitute canola seed meal or blood meal for urea. Sandra also uses some mushroom compost as a top-dressing and fish fertilizer is used for plants that show, by their yellow leaves, signs of nitrogen shortage. Plant debris is left on the mulch to decompose.

Pesticides are not used. Slugs are a major problem, which has been approached by growing enough produce for both slugs and humans, and by starting almost all the vegetables in soil blocks and then planting out the seedlings. Reemay and 4-inch-high (10-cm) wire window screening are both used successfully as slug barriers.

The result of the mulching program is a garden that requires no digging, very little weeding, and hardly any watering. The straw is readily available; the wood chips are a byproduct of a neighbor's tree-pruning business. The prunings are passed through a commercial-sized shredder to make the wood chips.

It is rare in gardening to have such consistency of application—the same mulches used on the same plot for over twelve years. So in February 1994, I asked for and was given permission to sample the soil.

Three samples were taken, one from unimproved grass-growing clay soil near the vegetable garden, and one each of soil from the straw-mulched and chip-mulched areas.

	UNIMPROVED		STRAW MULCH		CHIP MULCH		SUFFICIENCY LEVELS FOR VEGETABLES
Organic matter	7.5%	H	15.6%	H+	22.7%	VH	
pH	6.1	M	7.2	M+	6.7	M+	5.5 to 7.5
Nitrate (N)	5 ppm	VL	25 ppm	M–	12 ppm	L	30–50 ppm
Phosphorus (P)	132 ppm	H	401 ppm	VH	316 ppm	VH	75 ppm
Potassium (K)	181 ppm	H–	778 ppm	VH	537 ppm	VH	175 ppm
Magnesium	181 ppm	H	373 ppm	VH	368 ppm	VH	
Calcium	1296 ppm	H	3052 ppm	VH	2584 ppm	VH	
Sodium	3 ppm	VL	57 ppm	M	38 ppm	VL	
Sulphate	24 ppm	M	43 ppm	VH	41 ppm	VH	
Boron	.5 ppm	M	1.07 ppm	VH	2.06 ppm	VH	
Copper	1.0 ppm	M	2.0 ppm	H	2.7 ppm	H	
Iron	20 ppm	L	104.7 ppm	VH	251.8 ppm	VH	
Manganese	14.5 ppm	H	20 ppm	VH	34.2 ppm	VH	
Zinc	13.5 ppm	L	23.5 ppm	VH	23.8 ppm	VH	

ppm=parts per million   VH=very high   H=high   M=medium   L=low   VL=very low

The soil tests show the result of adding substantial quantities of organic material to a flat-lying, heavy clay soil. Except for the manganese reading, there is a dramatic increase in every tested element.

The tests confirm what is apparent to an observer: that the application of mulch with the addition of nitrogen fertilizer provides sufficient nutrients to more than meet average crop requirements. Or, put another way: gardeners who maintain high levels of organic material with mulches of straw or fine wood chips do not need to apply phosphorus (P), potassium (K) or trace elements on a regular basis.

PLANT HARDINESS
AND GROWING CONDITIONS

Plant hardiness is often thought of as a plant's susceptibility to low temperatures, but there are other factors involved. These include wind; moisture content of the soil and subsoil; the ability of the soil and subsoil to drain away winter rain quickly; the available nutrients in the soil; the amount of tender new growth on the plant; and the age and general health of the plant.

All these factors may be involved in the demise of one of your favorite plants. Without a plant pathology lab at your disposal the gardener's report on the cause of death will often be "from unknown causes."

One of the most obvious causes of plant loss is when freezing temperatures combined with high winds come early in the winter after a mild fall. This situation is particularly hard on broad-leafed evergreens. Bay and pineapple sage are borderline hardy at Ravenhill and are particularly affected (I have yet to see a plant book that discusses a plant's wind-chill hardiness rating).

There is some confusion as to how the moisture content of the soil and subsoil affects hardiness in conjunction with cold and wind. Some sources suggest watering evergreens just before a cold snap if the ground is dry; others say that if the ground is too wet, plants are more susceptible to cold. Both could be correct: the fine, shallow root hairs need to have some moisture as long as the topsoil is not too saturated and the deeper roots are not too wet.

In some cases the determining factor in winter survival may be the presence of disease. For example, rosemary is susceptible to a type of root fungus that shows up when parts of the branch system turn brown. Rosemary needs very good winter drainage and grows well when its roots have access to lime. Both these factors are probably involved in the hardiness of a particular plant, but there may also be a relationship between root fungus and winter-kill. It seems reasonable to assume that already diseased plants are more susceptible to winter-kill from poor drainage and/or malnutrition and that wet-rooted and/or undernourished plants are more susceptible to invasion by fungus present in the soil. Perhaps the presence of lime in the soil prevents the development of the root-destroying fungus. There are no clear answers here.

At Ravenhill, the watering of perennials is reduced to survival levels in early September. Fertilization with nitrogen also stops until the late winter (nitrogen fertilizer stimulates soft and sappy growth which may not have time to harden off before the winter arrives).

The soil is naturally supplied with potassium from the breakdown of the underlying granite rock. Having enough available potassium in the soil is said to be a factor in plant hardiness.

Tender plants are sited so that there is some shelter from north and northeast winds. In earlier years we did provide some winter protection by mulching globe artichokes and herb fennel, but do so no longer. The plants are either getting hardier with age or mulching was never necessary.

As all the plants are grown on a south-sloping hillside, good winter drainage has never been a problem. If the garden were flat, I would grow almost all the herbs and vegetables in raised beds or provide a drainage system to get rid of excess water quickly during winter rains.

Container plants are more vulnerable to freezing temperatures and cold winds. At Ravenhill, they are put in cold frames, placed underneath trees or put in a cold greenhouse in November.

Climate Modifiers

Several types of shelter can be used to protect tender plants, ranging from small portable cold frames to row covers and permanent greenhouse structures.

At Ravenhill, we use clear plastic tunnels for growing heat-loving basil in spring and summer; the tunnels could also be used for growing early spring and fall crops of salad greens, herbs and vegetables. Portable wood and plastic frames are used for growing early salad greens, corn, bush beans, cucumbers, zucchini, melons, eggplants and peppers. The frames are also used to grow winter salad greens and for protecting container plants from winter rain and frost.

The most ambitious and permanent of the climate modifiers are greenhouses. These can be anything from a homemade wood frame with plastic sheeting to the readymade aluminum and glass or plastic types. At Ravenhill, we have an 8 1/2- by 10 1/2-foot (2.6-by 3.2-m) unheated glass and aluminum greenhouse; it provides winter protection and spring growing and summer holding space for bays and basils, scented geraniums and other tender plants.

Floating row covers, such as Reemay, are used for a number of purposes. Reemay is a lightweight, spun polyester fabric that rests on the plants. It allows most of the sunlight and all the rain through, but creates a humid microclimate that helps the germination and growth of summer salad greens, radishes and carrots. It also provides a small amount of frost protection and, more importantly, protects herbs and vegetables from attacks by carrot rust fly, cabbage root fly, leaf miners and flea beetles. The edges of the cloth are pinned to the ground by soil or pieces of wood. The only drawback is that the fabric tears easily and rarely lasts for more than six months.

Open-topped frames can be placed over plants such as tomatoes. One frame we use at Ravenhill is constructed of wood with ultraviolet-light-treated polyethylene walls 30 inches (76 cm) high and no top. It is 17 feet (5 m) long and 4 feet (1.2 m) wide and encloses sixteen tomato plants. The clear plastic walls provide sufficient heat and protection from the wind to reliably ripen tomatoes in August and sometimes in early July.

Tunnel Construction

Our tunnels are made to fit over a 3 1/2-foot-wide (1-m) raised bed. The hoops are made from white PVC pipe, 1/2-inch (1.25 cm) in diameter. The PVC pipe comes in 20-foot (6-m) lengths and is cut into three equal parts. The hoops are spaced 5 feet (1.5 m) apart along the bed. A central wire or flexible plastic pipe is fastened to the top of each hoop and then fastened to a stake driven into the ground at each end of the tunnel. The tunnel is covered with ultraviolet-light-inhibited, clear, 4-mm polyethylene plastic sheeting. A three-hoop frame would require an 18-foot-long (5.5-m) sheet. If more height is required inside the tunnel, the ends of the hoops can be extended by driving into the ground a 12-inch-long (30-cm) piece of 3/4-inch (1.9 cm) PVC pipe and inserting the 1/2-inch (1.25-cm) pipe inside it.

The plastic sheeting is fastened with pliable plastic-covered wire to four wooden stakes driven in at the corners of the tunnel.

Ventilation is essential as soon as the sun appears, and is achieved by lifting up part of the downwind side of the tunnel sheet. Alternatively, small ventilation holes can be cut along the top of the sheeting to allow the escape of hot air and still provide adequate heat for growth.

To water, we unfasten one corner of the plastic sheet and use a watering wand.

The same tunnels have been used from April to July for the past ten years. The clear plastic is not quite as clear as it used to be, but there is little deterioration from sunlight. The tunnel cannot withstand high winds in an exposed location.

Cold Frame Construction

The main spring, fall and winter cold frame at Ravenhill is a movable wooden segmented box frame with a plastic top made of Coroplast, a type of twin-walled translucent plastic. The frames are stackable and can be built up to a height that suits the plants being grown.

The base frame measures 48 inches (1.2 m) by 44 inches (1 m) and is constructed of untreated 1 by 6 rough-cut cedar boards with 8-inch-long (20-cm) inside corner posts of 2 by 2 cedar. The corner posts are sharpened and project 5 1/2 inches (14 cm) into the ground. The posts and corners are nailed with 2 1/2-inch nails. Glueing and screwing would be stronger but nailing the posts allows a little flexibility, making them easier to stack.

The middle frame, or frames, are the same as the base except that the inside corner posts are 5 inches (13 cm) long and project 2 1/2 inches (6 cm) below the frame to fit into the frame below.

The sides of the top frame are cut on a slant to allow water to drain off the plastic top.

Coroplast can handle the weight of up to 6 inches (15 cm) of snow for this size of frame; larger frames would need a supporting strut. This type of plastic has a five-year guarantee; our cold frames have been used for nine years, and while the plastic has become more brittle, only one top is unusable.

The plastic lets in 75 percent of the solar energy, which seems to be adequate. The frames are not particularly airtight, but they do cut down greatly on air movement. On cloudy spring days the inside air temperature is 5 to 7°F (3 to 4°C) higher than the outside air.

The frames are light enough to be moved around easily, yet sturdy enough to withstand a strong wind. Ventilation is provided by lifting up one side of the top frame and resting two posts on the top of the lower frame. In gardens exposed to winter gales, it is advisable to weigh the top down with a rock.

Soil Blocks

For those plants that need an early start but won't germinate in cold soils, soil blocks are an excellent solution. Once the seedling is growing strongly it can be placed directly in the ground or potted up.

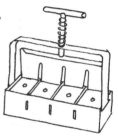

The blocks are made with a soil blocker, available from some garden stores and Lee Valley Tools (see Garden Supplies). The blocker compresses moistened potting soil into a 1 3/4-inch (4.5-cm) cube. The blocks are placed in a tray and covered with clear plastic until the first leaves appear. The plastic is then removed and the seedlings placed in a bright window. The blocks reduce the use of plastic plant pots, are quick and easy to make, reduce seed wastage and improve seed germination.

Raised Beds

One of the first things we did at Ravenhill was to make raised beds in an existing vegetable garden. We were mainly concerned with increasing the depth of soil, but it soon became obvious that there were many good reasons to garden with raised beds.

Soil in raised beds warms up more quickly and speeds up plant growth in the late winter and early spring. Raised beds can also solve problems of poor drainage (although improved drainage may not be an advantage in a hot, dry summer because it leads to increased water use. Raised beds surrounded by well-trodden paths can help deter slugs and snails.

We made our beds from 12 to 33 feet (3.7 to 10 m) long and 3 1/2 feet (1 m) wide. This width allows ready access to the middle of the bed from either side and allows us to cultivate the bed without walking on the soil and compacting it. The compaction of soil hugely increases the difficulty that tiny, near-surface plant roots have in extracting moisture and nutrition from the topsoil. One of the few rules around the farm is to never walk on the soil of any garden bed. Even the dogs quickly grasped the meaning of "off."

Our first beds were made by digging out the surrounding paths about 6 inches (15 cm) down and piling the earth on the beds. The beds were flat, with a small raised lip to prevent water from running down the sides. Remaking the high south, or downslope, side of the beds became a yearly chore. Eventually we shored up the south sides of some of the beds with 2- by 10-inch (5- by 25-cm) cedar planks, which reduced the annual labor, but led to an increase in the number of sow bugs (partially the result of increasing the amount of organic material in the soil).

PEST AND DISEASE CONTROL

One of the issues that faces every gardener is that of controlling pests and disease in the garden. It is sometimes tempting, when your most-prized plants are slowly (or quickly) succumbing to a pest or disease, to consider a quick chemical fix. But there is a growing awareness of the long-range environmental damage that may result from these solutions.

Environmental pollution takes place on two main levels. There is the obvious, fairly easily measured and not easily corrected level of nuclear fallout, smog, acid rain and oil spills. And there is another level where pollution causes changes in microorganisms and cell structure. It is here that environmental change is hard to detect and difficult to measure; its effects are sometimes irreversible and are often seen long after the original damage has occurred. There are a number of chemicals that are suspected of causing cell damage directly or indirectly, but the linkage of cause and effect has not yet been proven scientifically. To make it more difficult for the layperson, scientists differ among themselves over the potential harmful effects of various chemicals.

The chemicals, both organic and inorganic, that are released by gardeners and farmers into the environment are, in effect, a kind of experiment: the short-term results of these practices may be obvious but the long-term ones are not.

Agricultural chemicals are being primarily tested to determine whether they leave a residue in food products. Testing is carried out by the manufacturing companies and the test results are then examined by Agriculture Canada and Canada Food and Drug inspection. There are strict requirements for both the length of breakdown time and the amount of residue of the chemical.

The company manufacturing and testing the chemical may in some cases examine its effect on the cells of rats and on the tissue culture of human cells. But there are a number of problems with testing procedures. One is that the testing is done on a very pure sample; the same chemical is frequently not as pure when it is used in the garden and these impurities may not be tested. Second, the testing is carried out on the active chemical and not on the associated carriers. Third, testing is done for residues of the active chemical and little attention is paid to the effect of the chemical upon the microorganic life of the soil and the possibility that new compounds will form and enter the food chain.

Until there are adequate scientific and regulatory means of identifying the effects of chemicals and limiting the use of those that are dangerous, it makes sense to limit the exposure of any part of the food chain to potentially harmful chemicals. This is where all gardeners can play an important role in the reduction of chemical use.

Insect Controls

While there are a myriad pesticides to choose from, there are also many alternatives that do not rely on chemical aids. Insect controls at Ravenhill include encouraging beneficial insects by growing host plants, such as fennel, parsley and dill, in or near the vegetable garden. We are also careful not to destroy beneficial insects. For instance, wasps feed on the eggs of the cabbage butterfly and their nest near the vegetable garden is left undisturbed.

The whole subject of plants attracting and repelling animals, insects and other plants is fascinating but difficult to assess. Onions, shallots and garlic are said to discourage rabbits. French marigold supposedly repels a number of insects, including the asparagus beetle. A number of culinary herbs, according to Rodale's *Encyclopedia of Organic Gardening*, repel cabbage maggot (mints, rosemary and sage), aphids (mints, garlic and chives) as well as mites (garlic, chives) and flea beetles (garlic). This does not mean that the insects are not present, just that little damage is done.

Our experiments at Ravenhill have not been conclusive. We planted strong-smelling calendula around the asparagus patch to repel the asparagus beetle, but it didn't work. In another instance, we grow a number of members of the onion family around the vegetable garden, which is within 60 feet (18 m) of a large patch of blackberries that harbors rabbits, and the rabbits do not molest our lettuce.

Assessing the effectiveness of these measures is difficult because it's so hard to tell which is doing exactly what and to whom. Are the rabbits merely afraid of the dogs? We certainly have very few cabbage maggots in the garden, but is it due to the many wasps we encourage or some other factor?

A few common-sense practices in the garden can help reduce problems. To begin with, start with good, healthy stock, and make sure your plants are grown with all the essential nutrients, water and appropriate siting. Healthy plants that grow without check are better able to withstand attacks by insects.

Other measures include avoiding monoculture, or putting too many plants of the same type in too large a bed. Crop rotation is one of the most important ways to prevent the year-to-year buildup of insect pests. We also use varied cultural techniques, such as planting out seedlings (instead of sowing in place) to get the plants through an insect-vulnerable stage, and varied planting times. Planting out at different times may avoid the damaging cycles of certain insect pests, such as flea beetles and carrot rust fly. Barriers, such as Reemay, are especially effective for pests such as carrot rust fly, cabbage root maggot fly and flea beetles. If a plant is particularly susceptible to insect damage, we remove those parts that are attractive to the insect. For example, we pinch out the growth tips of fava beans when they are first attacked by the black fly.

Good garden cleanup practices can be invaluable. Dead plant material often harbors pests.

Finally, it's a good idea to grow lots of culinary herbs. The wonderful scents and flavors we prize in cooking are often oils developed by the plant to ward off the attentions of unwanted insects.

Disease Controls

At Ravenhill disease control starts with choosing plants suitable for the climate, the soil, the site and our cultivation techniques.

We also choose seeds and seedlings that are disease resistant, especially if the plant is susceptible, such as peas and tomatoes. For some plants that are susceptible to diseases, such as strawberries and grapes, we plant certified virus-free stock.

Certain basic principles of pest control also help control disease: it is important to grow plants without any checks to their growth from inadequate soil preparation, lack of water or an unsuitable site; avoid growing large areas of the same kind of plant; and rotate crops from year to year, especially potatoes, tomatoes and peppers, the onion family and brassicas (see Crop Rotation, below).

Watering methods are an important consideration in avoiding blight and fungus diseases. Avoid overhead watering and watering late in the day if plants are susceptible to mildew; some examples are bee balm, roses, and squash.

Clean up garden refuse and destroy or dispose of diseased plant material immediately.

Weed Controls

Adequate bed preparation, especially in removing every fragment of perennial weeds like Canada thistle, couch grass, sheep sorrel and small-leafed convolvulus is of the utmost importance in weed control. In the early years at the farm this meant clearing ground of ivy and periwinkle and leaving it clear for a summer before planting shrubs and perennial herbs.

Once the beds are established, continue to be vigilant about removing perennial weeds. Removing the thistles and couch grass from an established asparagus patch took two summers of consistent weeding.

Hoe and hand-pull weeds before they set seed. Pour boiling water on plants growing between bricks set in sand. Remove the seed heads from tall grasses growing on the edges of the garden, or maintain a mowed strip around the vegetable garden.

Hot compost or destroy weedy and seedy material.

Use strong garden fabric or plastic edging. Plastic edging works well where perennial grasses can invade beds or earth paths. Plastic edging, 18 inches (45 cm) wide, has been used to surround an area cleared of St. Johns wort; this has now been in place for five years without a serious reinvasion.

At Ravenhill, there is a heavy invasion of tree roots in parts of the garden, in some areas restricting the kinds of plants we can grow. Rosemary competes well, as do oregano, thyme and mint. Plants that need a lot of water, like raspberries, globe artichokes and asparagus, do not compete as well but can be grown in raised beds. The wild native plum spreads by suckering and is proving a nuisance, but that is mainly because it hasn't been dug up consistently.

One of the many beneficial effects of mulch is weed control. A 6-inch (15-cm) layer of mulch prevents the germination of most weeds. A 2-inch (5-cm) layer makes any weeds that do grow much easier to pull by hand.

Finally, be persistent. In our vegetable garden the beds are well defined by hard earth paths and a few wooden edges and grass strips. The definition of the beds seems to be of help in the psychology of weeding: one bed at a time, one day at a time.

Crop Rotation

At Ravenhill, crop rotation is primarily used for the prevention of disease and avoiding the build-up of insect pests that feed on specific families of vegetables.

We don't grow members of the onion family (chives, shallots, garlic and leeks) in the same place more than one year in three. The same strategy is used for members of the Brassica family (which includes cabbage, radish, kale, arugula and broccoli), the Solanum family (tomatoes, eggplants, potatoes and peppers), corn, and the squash family (melons, cucumbers, pumpkins and zucchini).

The most important nutrient rotation (other than growing green manures as part of the rotation) is that of the nitrogen fixers—the legumes. Peas and beans are grown in beds that will next hold heavy nitrogen users, like lettuce, spinach, squash and corn. After harvesting, the roots of legumes are left in the soil to decompose. Secondary nutrient rotations, like rotating high phosphorus users (squash family) and high potassium users (onion family), are less important, partly because of the high levels of both phosphorus and potassium in Ravenhill's soil and also because we use compost to build up the soil for both families prior to planting.

THE SUSTAINABLE GARDEN

Beyond the ideal of the Organic Garden lies the Sustainable Garden.

As the levels of water and air and soil pollution rise on Planet Earth, so the question of the sustainability of human life on Earth grows in people's consciousness.

On a small scale, the garden mirrors some of the problems caused by environmental changes made in the name of economic progress. The garden is one area where the owner has both the responsibility and the power to make positive changes.

A gardener's responsibility was once limited to the fences of the property, just as responsibility for a nation used to stop at the frontier. Responsibility in the garden now means being aware of changes to the soil that may affect the food chain in a negative way, either through obvious air, water or soil pollution, or at a cellular level.

Sustainability in the garden, at its simplest level, means being independent of outside supplies of fertilizer and still maintaining the organic matter and nutrients at sufficient levels for crop production.

One approach to this problem has been pioneered by John Jeavons, the author of *How to Grow More Vegetables*. His work suggests that in order to grow a sustainable garden of any size you need a comparable area in green manures, which would provide both organic matter and nitrogen. The green manures would then be an integral part of the garden rotation.

The soil test results from Sandra Holloway's mulch garden show that the vegetable garden is dependent on outside sources for the large quantities of straw and/or wood chips, as well as a liberal supply of nitrogen (primarily from urea, most of which is obtained from natural gas) and spot applications of fish fertilizer. Ravenhill brings in straw, alfalfa, fish fertilizer, blood meal, rock phosphate, dolomite lime and occasional loads of horse and cow manure, as well as bagged feed for the chickens and sheep. To achieve the goal of the sustainable garden, we would have to grow sufficient organic matter and nitrogen-fixing plants to replace the material currently being brought in.

The mixed cattle, grain and vegetable farms of nineteenth- and early twentieth-century Europe and North America were largely self-sustaining as far as organic matter and fertilizers were concerned. In another example, the market gardeners outside London, England, the railways and London stables had an interesting symbiotic relationship. The growers in the rural areas used the horse manure generated in the city's stables. The railways carried the horse manure out to the growers and the fresh produce into the London markets.

This shifting or redistribution of resources is, while not strictly sustainable gardening, a common-sense approach to using garden additives. Another, related issue for gardeners is the distinction between renewable and nonrenewable resources. It is easy to claim that straw, blood and bone meal, horse, chicken and cow manure, and maybe fish fertilizer are renewable resources. It is hard to make the same claim for peat moss, urea and rock phosphate.

The ideals of the sustainable garden and even of using only renewable resources may be out of reach for most gardeners, but the underlying principles surely bear discussion and experimentation.

CULINARY HERBS
FOR SPECIFIC PLACES
AND PURPOSES

Rock garden conditions (poor soil): calendula, chamomile (German), curry, hyssop, lavender, marjoram (hardy), oregano (Italian and Greek), rosemary (upright), sage (garden and 'Holt's Mammoth'), savory (winter), thyme (lemon, French and caraway).

Vegetable garden (good soil): basil, borage, chives, cilantro, dill, fennel, horseradish, lovage, onion (Welsh), parsley, salad burnet, savory (summer), sorrel, tarragon, thyme (lemon).

Flower garden (average soil): anise hyssop, basil (opal), bay, bee balm, calamint, calendula, chamomile (German), chives, chives (garlic), curry, dill, fennel, hyssop, lavender, lovage, marjoram, oregano, rosemary (upright), sage (garden), salad burnet, thyme (lemon and French).

Herbs that can be left undisturbed for four or more years: bay, curry, fennel, lavender, lemon balm, lovage, marjorams, oregano, rosemary, sage, savory (winter), sorrel, tarragon, thyme (French).

Gardens that get little direct sun: borage, calendula, chervil, chives, cilantro, dill, fennel, horseradish, lemon balm, lovage, mint, onion (Welsh), parsley.

Grow well in containers: anise hyssop, basil, bay, calendula, chives, chives (garlic), hyssop, lemon grass, marjorams, mints, oregano, parsley, rosemary, savory (winter), tarragon, thymes, verbena (lemon).

Good ground covers: chamomile (Roman), lavender, marjoram (hardy), mint (Corsican), oregano, salad burnet, savory (winter), thymes.

Winter and summer use: curry, hyssop, onion (Welsh), parsley, rosemary, sage, savory (winter), sorrel, thyme.

Edging and hedging: chives, curry plant, hyssop, lavender, marjoram, rosemary (upright), savory (winter), thyme (lemon).

Herbes de Provence (mixed dried herbs used for barbecue and flavoring stews and soups): thyme, rosemary, oregano, marjoram (sweet), basil and savory (summer); savory (winter) and lavender are sometimes added.

Bouquet Garni (a small bundle of herbs tied together or placed in a cheesecloth bag, used for flavoring soups, stocks or sauces, and removed before serving): parsley, French thyme and bay leaves; celery, sage, cloves or savory may be added.

Edible Flowers: anise hyssop, bee balm, basil, borage, calendula, chives, chives (garlic), cilantro, dill, fennel, lavender, marjoram, oregano, sage (garden and pineapple), thymes.

SEED CATALOGS
AND SPECIALTY
NURSERIES

Both cook and gardener are using and growing more and more kinds of culinary herbs and vegetables. Gardeners are demanding seeds that grow well in specific climates, and cooks are demanding fresher, tastier produce with no contamination from herbicides, fungicides or pesticides. Some seed houses are responding faster than others to changes in demand. Those listed below meet most of our requirements at Ravenhill.

Individuals can bring plants across the border by filling out forms and having the plants inspected. Richters ships well-packaged plants across Canada and to the U.S.A. Nichols does not ship plants to Canada. All seed houses mail seeds across the border. Canadians wishing to import plants from the United States should check with Agriculture Canada for the latest regulations. In Vancouver, call 666-2891; the Victoria number is 338-3421.

Seed Houses

Abundant Life, P.O. Box 772, Port Townsend, WA 98368. All seeds are open-pollinated (no hybrids) and are not treated with fungicides. The catalog is good for most vegetables, excellent for tomatoes, beans and edible seeds. Fair to good for culinary herbs. Most seeds have undergone trials in the Pacific Northwest.

The Cook's Garden, P.O. Box 535, Londonderry, Vermont, 05148. Excellent selection of vegetable seeds; many unusual types, especially from Europe. Good selection of basils, fairly good for other herbs. A few herb plants.

Nichols Garden Nursery, 1190 North Pacific Highway, Albany, OR, 97321-4598. Excellent selection of vegetable seeds. Good selection of herb seeds and herb plants. Almost all seeds are untreated and grow successfully in the Willamette Valley of Oregon.

Richters, Goodwood, Ontario L0C 1A0. The best selection of culinary herbs, both seeds and plants. Very good small selection of unusual vegetable seeds.

Salt Spring Seeds, P.O. Box 33, Ganges, B.C. V0S 1E0. All seeds grown organically on Salt Spring Island. Superb selection of beans, amaranth and heirloom wheat. Good selection of tomatoes. Excellent selection of garlic in September.

Shepherd's Garden Seeds, 6116 Highway 9, Felton, CA 95018. Excellent selection of vegetable seeds, many European types, great salad greens. Very good basils. Fairly good on other culinary herb seeds, plus a few herb plants.

Territorial Seeds, 200 - 8475 Ontario Street, Vancouver, B.C. V5X 3E8; and P.O. Box 157, 20 Palmer Avenue, Cottage Grove, Oregon 97424. Excellent selection of locally tested vegetable seeds along with sound and detailed growing advice for Pacific Northwest gardens. Standard culinary herb seed list.

Specialty Nurseries

The following specialty nurseries are good sources of culinary herb plants in the Pacific Northwest.

Barn Owl Nursery, 22999 SW Newland Road, Wilsonville, OR 97070. Open April to July and mid-September to mid-December; telephone 503-672-7766.

The Bellingham Garden Spot, King and Alabama Street, Bellingham, WA 98225. Open year round; telephone 206-676-5480.

Cedarbrook Herb Farm, 986 Sequim Avenue South, Sequim, WA 98382. Open March to end of December; telephone 206-683-7733.

Dutchmill Herbfarm, 6640 NW Marsh Road, Forest Grove, OR 97116. Open Wednesday to Saturday; telephone 503-357-0924.

Easy Acres Herb Farm, 12063 - 64th Avenue, Surrey, B.C. V3W 1W5. Open daily; telephone 604-596-8485.

Elderflower Farm, 501 Callahan Road, Roseburg, OR 97470. Open summer to fall—call ahead; telephone 503-672-7766.

Fairie Herb Gardens, 6236 Elm Street SE, Tumwater, WA 98501. Open March 15 to September 30; telephone 206-754-9249.

Fairlight Gardens Nursery, 30904 - 164th SE, Auburn, WA 98002. Open April to November; telephone 206-631-8932.

Foxglove Herb Farm, 6617 Rosedale Street, Gig Harbor, WA 98335. Open mid-April to September; telephone 206-851-7477.

Goodwin Creek's Secret Garden, 154 1/2 Oak Street, Ashland, OR 97520. Open April to July; mid-September to mid-December, Wednesdays and Sundays; telephone 503-488-3308.

Happy Valley Herbs, 3497 Happy Valley Road, RR 1, Victoria, B.C. V9C 2Y2. Open April to end of September; telephone 604-474-5767.

Hazelwood Farm, 13576 Adshead Road, RR 1, Ladysmith, B.C. V0R 2E0. Open April to end of September, Wednesday to Sunday; October to December, weekends; telephone 604-245-8007.

Herban Renewal, 10437 - 19th Avenue SW, Seattle, WA 98146. Open April through October, Thursday to Saturday; telephone 206-243-8821.

The Herbfarm, 32804 Issaquah-Fall City Road, Fall City, WA 98024. Open year round; telephone 206-784-2222.

The Herb Gardener, 13450 NE 100th Street, Kirkland, WA 98033-5252. Open year round, by appointment; telephone 206-822-8580.

House of Whispering Firs, 20080 SW Jaquith Road, Newberg, OR 97132. Open year round; telephone 503-628-3695.

Hummingbird Farm, 2041 N Zylstra Road, Oak Harbor, WA 98277. Open February to end of December; telephone 206-679-5044.

Lowland Herb Farm, 5685 Lickman Road, Sardis/Chilliwack, B.C. V2R 1A6. Open Friday and Saturday, March to October or by appointment; telephone 604-858-4216.

Meadow View Country Gardens, 2315 Upper River Road Loop, Grants Pass, OR 97526. Open Monday to Saturday; telephone 503-471-8841.

Nichols Garden Nursery, 1190 SW Pacific, Albany, OR 97321. Open Monday to Saturday; telephone 503-928-9280.

Ravenhill Herb Farm, 1330 Mt. Newton X-Road, Saanichton, B.C. V8M 1S1. Open April to end of August, Sundays only; telephone 604-652-4024.

Semiahmoo Herb Farm, 16855 - 14th Avenue, White Rock, B.C. V4B 5A8. Open daily from April to August; weekends all year; telephone 604-538-2727.

Silver Bay Herb Farm, 9151 Tracyton Boulevard, Bremerton, WA 98310. Open March to end of December; telephone 206-692-1340.

The Wallingford Garden Spot, 45th and Wallingford in the Wallingford Center, Seattle, WA. Open year round; telephone 206-547-5137.

Whitegate Farm, 3700 Kingburne Drive, Cobble Hill, B.C. V0R 1L0. Open May to end of September, by appointment; telephone 604-743-7106.

Windy River Farm, 348 Hussey Lane, Grants Pass, OR 97527. Open year round, by appointment; telephone 503-476-8979.

Garden Supplies

Lee Valley Tools, 1080 Morrison Drive, Ottawa, Ontario K2H 8K7. Catalog contains garden supplies, including a soil-block maker. Lee Valley Tools ships to the U.S.

FURTHER READING AND REFERENCE

Books

Adams, James. *Landscaping with Herbs*. Portland: Timber Press, 1987.

Colebrook, Binda. *Winter Gardening in the Maritime Northwest*. Everson, WA: Maritime Publications, 1984.

The Encyclopedia of Organic Gardening. Emmaus, PA: Rodale Press, 1978.

Foster, Stephen. *Herbal Bounty*. Salt Lake City: Peregrine Smith Books, 1984.

Harrington, Geri. *Grow Your Own Chinese Vegetables*. Vermont: Garden Way, 1984.

Jacobs, E.M. Betty. *Growing and Using Herbs Successfully*. Vermont: Garden Way, 1976.

Jason, Dan. *Greening the Garden*. Philadelphia: New Society Publishers, 1991.

Jeavons, John. *How to Grow More Vegetables.* Palo Alto: Ecology Action of the Midpeninsula, 1974.

McNeilan, Ray, and Micheline Ronningen. *Pacific Northwest Guide to Home Gardening.* Portland: Timber Press, 1982.

Ogden, Shepherd. *Step by Step Organic Vegetable Gardening.* New York: Harper Collins, 1992.

Rodale's Illustrated Encyclopedia of Herbs. Emmaus, PA: Rodale Press, 1987.

Salter, P.J., Bleasdale, J.K.A. and Others. *Know and Grow Vegetables.* Oxford: Oxford University Press, 1979.

Solomon, Steve. *Growing Vegetables West of the Cascades.* Seattle: Sasquatch Press, 1989.

Stevens, Elaine, and Dagmar Hungerford, Doris Fancourt-Smith, Jane Mitchell, Ann Buffam. *The Twelve Month Gardener.* Vancouver: Whitecap Books, 1991.

Sturtevant, E. Louis. Ed. U.P. Hedrick. *Sturtevant's Edible Plants of the World.* New York: Dover, 1972.

Sunset. *Western Garden Book.* Menlo Park: Lane Publishing, 1988.

Tarrant, David. *Pacific Gardening Guide.* Vancouver: Whitecap Books, 1989.

Vilmorin-Andrieux. *The Vegetable Garden.* Berkeley, CA: Ten Speed, 1993. (This was first published in English in 1885 and is a wonderful account of pre-chemical-revolution growing.)

Magazines

The Herb Companion. Bimonthly. (Interweave Press, 201 East Fourth Street, Loveland, CO 80537, U.S.A.)

The Island Grower. Ten issues a year. (Greenheart Pub., R.R. 4, Sooke, B.C. V0S 1N0, Canada).

Organic Gardening. Nine issues a year (Rodale Press, 33 E. Minor Street, Emmaus, PA 18098, U.S.A).

INDEX

Main entries are shown in **bold**.